101 ESSENTIAL TIPS

TENNIS

PRO

101 ESSENTIAL TIPS

TENNIS

Paul Douglas

DORLING KINDERSLEY

London • New York • Stuttgart • Moscow

A DORLING KINDERSLEY BOOK

Editor Simon Adams
Art Editor Alison Shackleton
Series Editor Charlotte Davies
Managing Art Editor Amanda Lunn
Production Controller Louise Daly

PUBLISHER'S NOTE
The instructions in this book are assumed for right-handed players, and where appropriate should be reversed for left-handed players.

First published in Great Britain in 1995 by
Dorling Kindersley Limited,
9 Henrietta Street, London WC2E 8PS

A CIP catalogue record for this book is available from the British Library

ISBN 0-7513-0229-5

Computer page make-up by Alison Shackleton
Text film output by The Right Type, Great Britain
Reproduced by Colourscan, Singapore
Printed and bound by Graphicom, Italy

101 ESSENTIAL TIPS

PREPARING TO PLAY

1 WHAT TO WEAR

Choose tennis clothes that are comfortable to wear and made of light, washable fabrics. Shorts and skirts should not be too tight around the waistband, and shirts must allow your shoulders and arms freedom to move. It is advisable to wear socks with cushioned soles and heels for added comfort and protection.

MEN'S TENNIS KIT

WOMEN'S TENNIS KIT

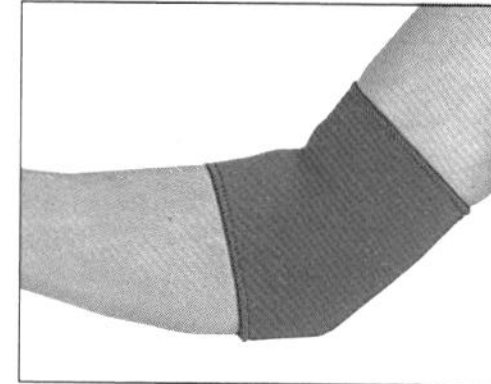

NEOPROPENE SUPPORT
A flexible bandage provides warmth and support to a strained elbow.

2 Footwear

Protect your feet and improve your footwork on the court by choosing good tennis shoes. They must provide flexibility and stability and give support to your insteps, ankles, and Achilles tendons.

Ideally, you should select shoes to suit your game and the type of court on which you play most often. Different court surfaces require different soles: smooth soles for indoors, pimpled for grass, and herringbone for general use. If you can only afford one pair of shoes, then cross-trainers are good as they can be used for almost any sport.

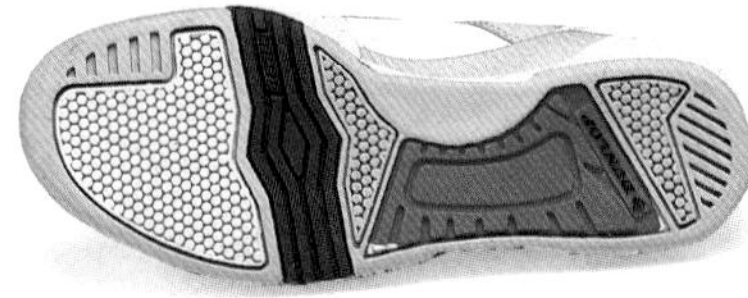

All-purpose Shoe
This tennis shoe has a multi-purpose sole that allows the player to perform well on grass, clay, or asphalt surfaces.

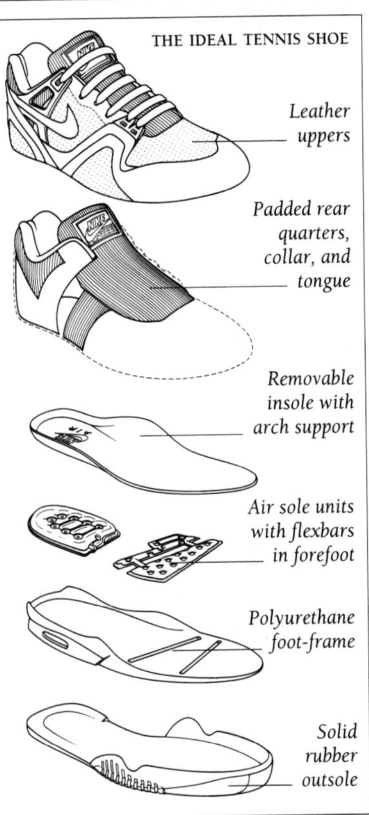

3 Which Tennis Balls?

Tennis balls have to undergo rigorous testing procedures before they are approved for tournament play. Always choose leading brand balls that are sold in pressurized cans, as it is bad for your game to play with inferior tennis balls. If you are performing exercises with your partner or working out using a ball machine, second-grade balls are acceptable.

TENNIS BALLS

4 Choosing the Right Racket

Rackets come in many different shapes and sizes. Most are variations on the wide-bodied type. These rackets are light and strong, and more powerful than slimmer-bodied models. Their streamlined head and broad dimensions guarantee better manoeuvrability and stiffness. When buying a new racket, choose one that feels right for your grip. Beginners might like to select a cheaper model before buying a more powerful frame.

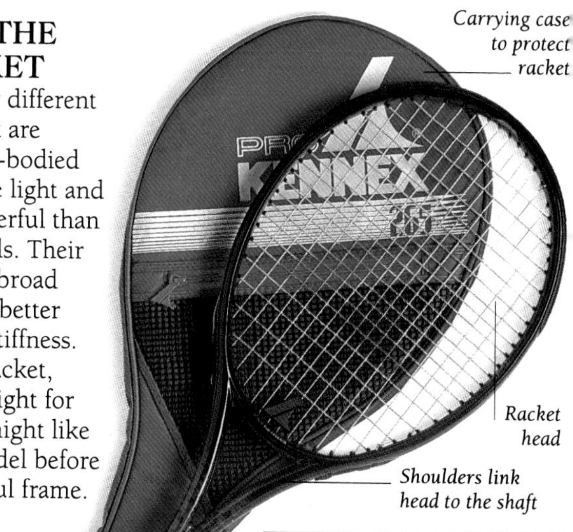

Materials
The days of wooden rackets are over, as modern rackets are now made of Kevlar, graphite, fibreglass, and boron, combining flex with strength. Powerful players require stiffer frames than touch players.

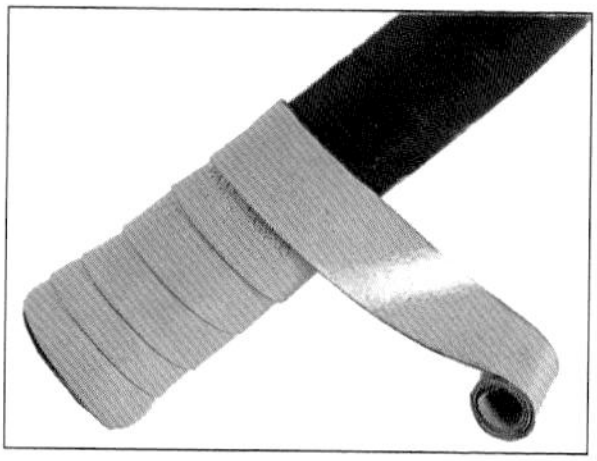

Carrying case to protect racket

Racket head

Shoulders link head to the shaft

Shaft disperses vibration from the head

Handle is often padded for protection

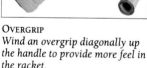

Overgrip
Wind an overgrip diagonally up the handle to provide more feel in the racket.

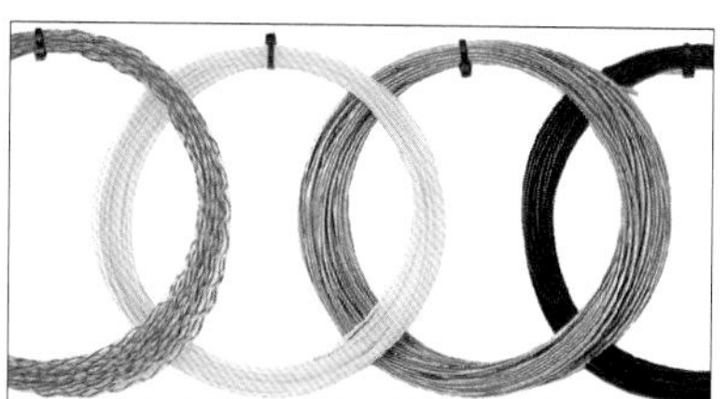

Racket strings

5 Which Strings?

Racket strings must be woven in a uniform pattern in the racket frame to ensure a flat hitting surface. There are two basic types of synthetic strings – monofilament and multifilament. Choose the latter as they are generally superior.

6 IMPROVING YOUR BALL CONTROL

Practise altering the angle of the racket face for different shots when hitting the ball by bouncing the ball up off the strings, then flipping the racket head over so that the next bounce comes off the other surface. A more difficult exercise is to bounce the ball off the edge or beam of the racket. Both drills develop control and strengthen your wrist.

Keep your eye on the ball at all times

Keep grip very steady and make slight upward movements of racket head to keep control of ball

BEAM BOUNCE

Watch ball closely

Use a natural grip and hold racket out before bouncing ball up off strings

Stand with feet shoulder-width apart and knees slightly flexed

STRING BOUNCE

7 BASIC BALL SENSE

Judging the flight of the ball as it comes towards you is an essential skill, and one that you can improve with a series of simple exercises.

- Throw a ball back and forth with a partner; catch it before it bounces. To develop your ball sense, bounce the ball to each other and catch it.
- Stretch your abilities by throwing two balls between yourself and your partner simultaneously.
- Use the palm of your hand to hit a ball thrown by your partner. This will develop your basic ground-stroke timing of hitting the falling ball between knee and waist height.

8 JOGGING & STRETCHING

Warm up before you play. It helps avoid injury, makes you feel mentally more like playing, and improves your performance. Begin with a gentle jog to raise your pulse rate, and spend 10 to 20 seconds on each exercise, first on one leg or side, then the other as appropriate. Take it easy and enjoy the stretch. Go through your routine again, holding each stretch slightly longer. Playing requires dynamic movement, so always jog and stretch first. Spend 15 minutes stretching.

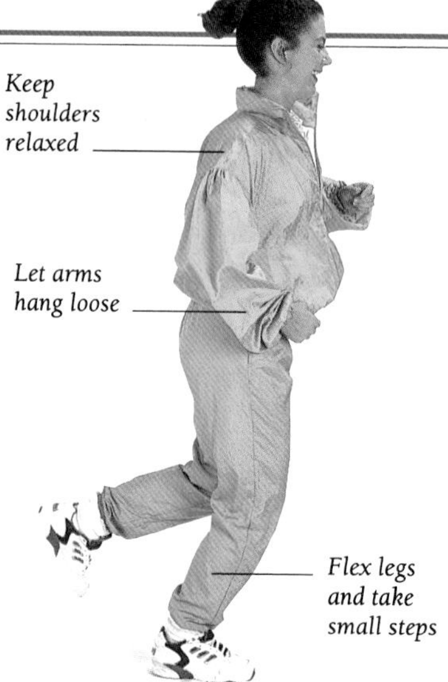
Keep shoulders relaxed
Let arms hang loose
Flex legs and take small steps

1 Slowly jog around the court up to five times to warm up your body. On the last two circuits, add side-skips and running backwards.

Rest head on arms if you wish
Stand about 30 cm (1 ft) from wall and lean towards it

4 Stretch your middle and lower leg by leaning against a wall with your right leg stretched backwards. Move your hips forwards and stretch.

Keep legs flat on the ground

5 To stretch your stomach muscles, lie flat on your stomach with your arms straight out in front of you. Pull yourself upright onto your palms.

Keep your right leg extended backwards

As you raise and lower hips, press body weight forwards

Pull hips forwards and heel tight in towards buttocks

Keep left leg straight to support body weight as you bend right knee

2 To stretch your upper leg, take a step forwards with your left leg, bending your knee and keeping it above your ankle. Lower hips and press forwards.

3 Stretch your front upper leg by placing your left palm against a wall, bending your right knee, and gripping your foot with your right hand.

Keep back horizontal
Rest right hand behind you
Place left elbow outside and above right knee to stop body twisting back
Keep left leg straight

6 To stretch your arms and wrists, place your hands on the floor with your fingers pointing towards your knees with your thumbs outside.

7 Stretch your body by putting your left leg on the ground and your right foot behind your left knee. Turn and look over your right shoulder.

9 Becoming Fit for Tennis

For strength and general fitness, follow a routine of body resistance exercises. For stamina, run at a steady rate for a kilometre (half a mile) every other day. Gradually run faster and increase your distance. Speed is vital too, so do some shuttle runs on court, sprinting between sidelines. For suppleness, do the stretching routine daily.

Hold for a second or two and then lower gently
Keep knees slightly flexed
Keep head up and shoulders back
Use arms to balance yourself
Keep legs slightly flexed
As you leap, pull knees up sharply towards chest

Buddy Training
Try this exercise with a partner. Stand back to back and interlock arms at the elbow. Then flex your knees, bend forwards from the waist, and lift your partner onto your back. Buddy exercises build strength.

1 For a double-knee jump, stand with your feet together. Crouch down and then leap into the air, bringing your knees up to your chest.

Bend knees
Keep feet flat on ground
Always keep one shoulder on the ground
Do not touch floor with your feet
Keep head flat on floor
Keep back straight and head up

2 For effective sit-ups, lie on the floor with your hands behind your head. Keep looking up as you raise your upper body by 45°.

3 Lie flat with your legs slightly raised. Bring your left elbow and right knee up towards each other.

4 To strengthen your lower stomach, lie flat with knees flexed and raise your legs to about 45°. Lower them slowly.

5 For press-ups, support your weight with your palms under your shoulders. Bend your arms and, without letting your legs touch the floor, lower your chest to the floor and then push up and repeat.

On the Court

10 The court

You need to know the court, its markings, surfaces, and net in order to get the best out of a game of tennis. Tennis lines are boundary lines and are named according to their function. The baselines and sidelines limit the depth and width of your drives and volleys, while the service lines restrict the depth of your service.

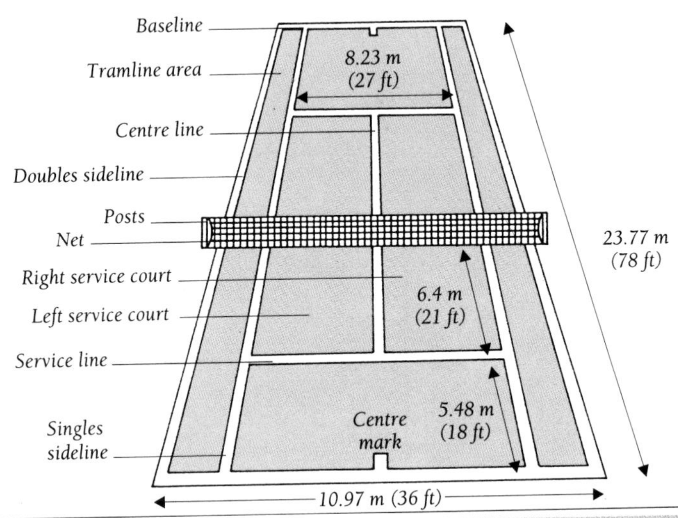

11 Court surfaces

There are four main court surfaces. Each of them produces different conditions of play and has a marked effect on your game. Experience will teach you which one you prefer.

- Grass is a fast-playing surface but is hard to maintain; artificial grass can be either fast or slow.
- Clay produces a slow game.
- Cement results in a fast or slow game, depending on its texture.
- Asphalt is slow but plays faster when the surface is painted.

12 THE NET

The net is more than just a barrier strung across the middle of the court: it also dictates your strokeplay and the type of shot you play. It provides problems for every shot and your task is to find the best solution for getting the ball over the net and placing it where it may force a weak return or win the point outright. Your opponent has similar problems to solve.

NET DICTATES PLAY
Because the net is 16 cm (6 in) lower in the centre than at the posts, play most shots over the middle of the net.

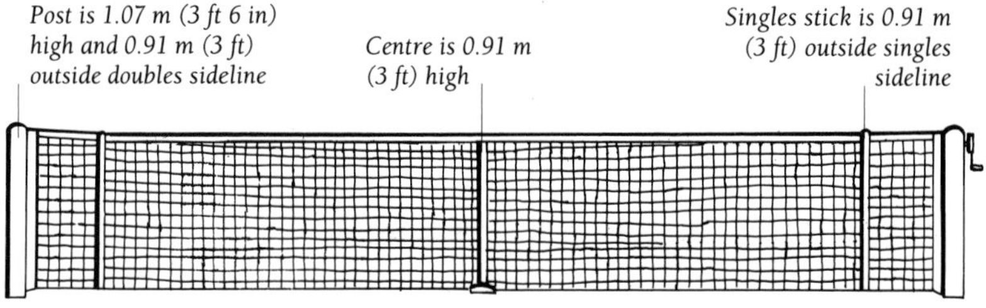
Post is 1.07 m (3 ft 6 in) high and 0.91 m (3 ft) outside doubles sideline
Centre is 0.91 m (3 ft) high
Singles stick is 0.91 m (3 ft) outside singles sideline

THE TENNIS NET

13 MENTAL SKILLS

Tennis is not just a game of physical ability, techniques, and tactics. As you gain in experience, you will discover that 75 per cent of the game is in the mind. Develop these skills to help your game.

- Concentration: Learn to focus your attention like a champion.
- Self-belief: Build up your self-confidence by visualizing success.
- Motivation: The extent of your desire to play and succeed is the measure of the progress you make.

14 MENTAL TRAINING

With mind-training exercises you can improve your mental skills in the same way as you practise on court to improve your game.

- Visualize yourself as a calm player in control of your game, and repeat a short phrase to inspire confidence.
- Set yourself goals to increase your motivation. Make them challenging, attainable, and performance-related.
- Practise concentrating – on your opponent's serve, or on the height of the ball as it crosses the net.

15 How the ball travels

When you first play groundstrokes, anticipating the flight of the ball after the bounce can be difficult. Judge where the ball will bounce on your side of the court, but avoid rushing towards it. Position yourself behind, and a comfortable distance from, the bounce point in order to control your return. The service also has two flights; the volley only one.

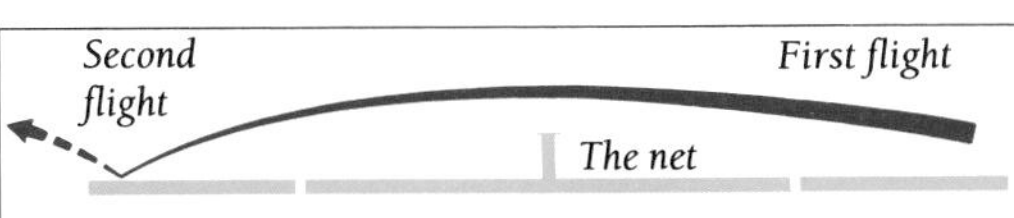

The Flight of the Ball
A ball has two flights: the first as it leaves your opponent's racket, the second after it bounces on your side of the net.

16 The ready position

To return the ball well you need good judgment and effective receiving skills. To develop these, start from an alert and stable ready position. Face the net with your weight on the balls of your feet and your racket held centrally in order to allow easy play on either side of your body.

From the Side
Bend to get your eyes in line with the shot. Keep your elbows away from your body for freedom of movement.

Watch your opponent play the ball to anticipate its speed and direction

Support racket head by lightly holding it at the throat

Stand with feet shoulder-width apart for stability and with knees flexed to lower your centre of gravity

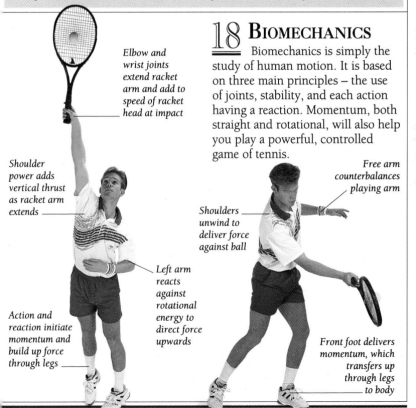

17 WHEN TO HIT THE BALL

You must know exactly when and where your racket head should make contact with the ball. This will enable you to position your body in relation to the ball to ensure perfect timing and control.

- For groundstrokes, play the ball between knee and waist height. When serving, hit the falling ball with your racket arm extended overhead. For volleys, hit the ball between waist and shoulder height.
- While a drive or service is played at a racket-arm's distance, a volley is played closer to the body.
- In relation to your body, the ball should be opposite your leading hip for forehand, ahead of your leading hip for backhand, and in front of you for both volleys and services.

Elbow and wrist joints extend racket arm and add to speed of racket head at impact

Shoulder power adds vertical thrust as racket arm extends

Left arm reacts against rotational energy to direct force upwards

Action and reaction initiate momentum and build up force through legs

18 BIOMECHANICS

Biomechanics is simply the study of human motion. It is based on three main principles – the use of joints, stability, and each action having a reaction. Momentum, both straight and rotational, will also help you play a powerful, controlled game of tennis.

Free arm counterbalances playing arm

Shoulders unwind to deliver force against ball

Front foot delivers momentum, which transfers up through legs to body

19 The importance of your grip

How you hold the racket determines how you play the game, for the feel that you get from the ball after it hits your racket is communicated to you through your grip.

- The basic grip is the Eastern Forehand grip. Shake hands with your racket, with your palm behind the handle, for a comfortable grip that gives you maximum strength to hit an approaching ball.
- As your playing becomes more advanced, you may require different grips. These will be introduced to you with each new stroke you learn.

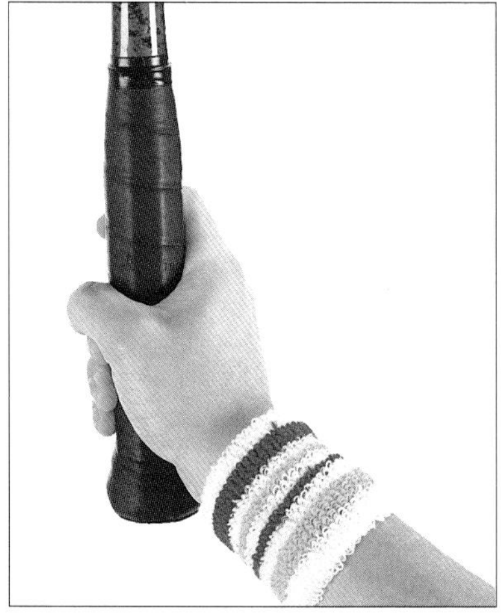

EASTERN FOREHAND GRIP

20 How the ball hits the racket

The angle of your racket face to the ball has a direct bearing on the outcome of any shot. The ball stays on your strings for about five-thousandths of a second and goes exactly where your racket's strings are aiming. For almost every shot, you should keep your racket face to within five degrees of the vertical (lob and drop shots excepted).

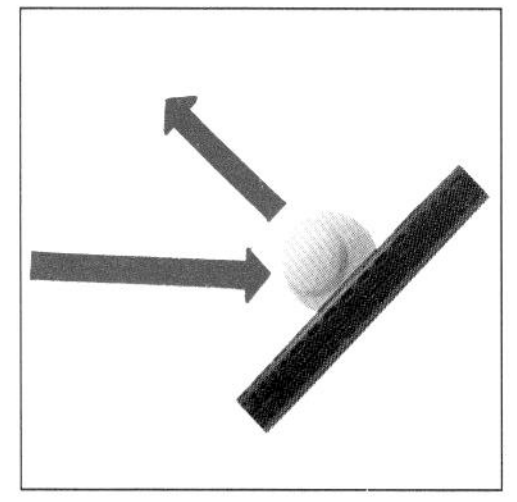

Open Face
An open racket face plays the ball upwards and encourages it to spin backwards.

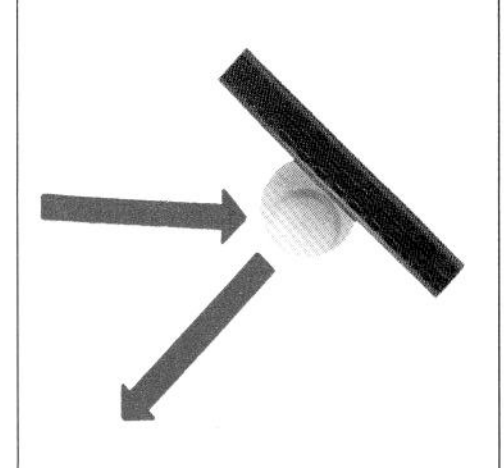

Closed Face
A closed racket face plays the ball downwards and encourages it to spin forwards.

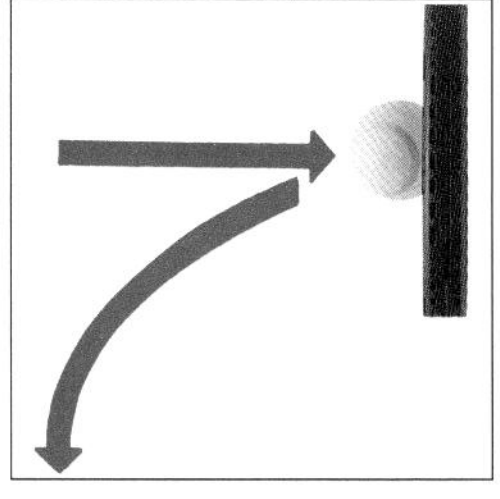

Flat Face
A flat racket face plays the ball straight ahead before gravity pulls it downwards.

21 USING SPIN

Spin, that is the way a ball rotates, has a considerable effect on how a ball travels through the air and bounces. The spin itself will be affected by whether the ball bounces off the court or your racket strings. Experiment with the three types of spin and see the effect each one has on the shot.

When serving with slice, angle racket face slightly and hit up and across back of ball from right to left to produce right-hand sidespin

SLICE SERVICE

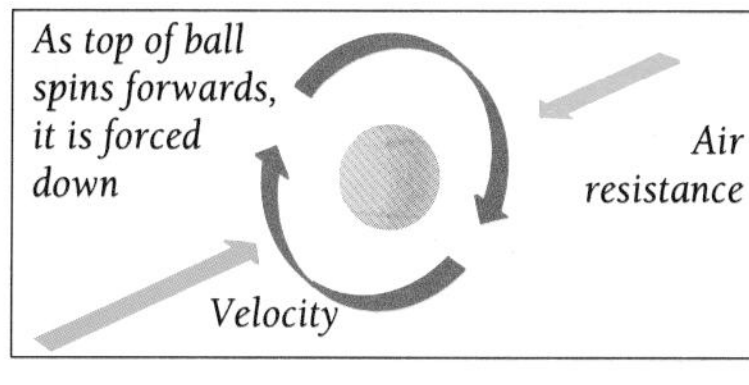
As top of ball spins forwards, it is forced down
Air resistance
Velocity

TOPSPIN
When you play topspin shots, aim higher over the net than you would when playing a basic drive.

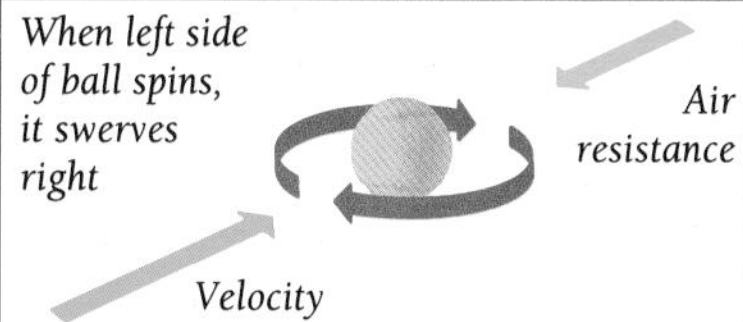
When left side of ball spins, it swerves right
Air resistance
Velocity

SIDESPIN
Sidespin is used for slice serving. Combined with topspin, it produces the topspin service that kicks and swerves.

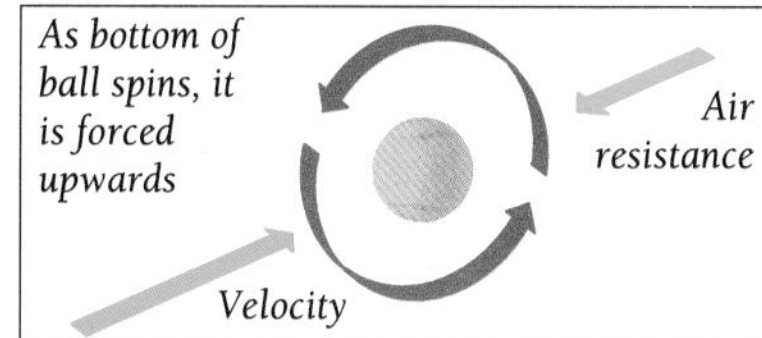
As bottom of ball spins, it is forced upwards
Air resistance
Velocity

UNDERSPIN
Lobbing apart, underspin shots travel low over the net. Underspin can be combined with sidespin in approach-shot play.

22 DOUBLE-COLOURED BALLS

To recognize easily which type of spin you have applied, try practising with double-coloured balls. Note the effect that each type of spin has on the flight of the ball.

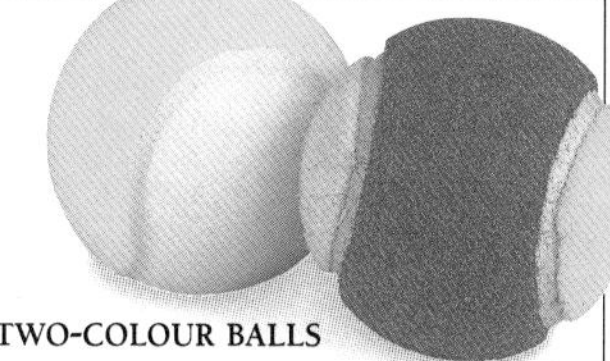

TWO-COLOUR BALLS

23 CALLING THE SHOTS

A stroke is the action of hitting the ball, while a shot describes the flight and eventual destination of the ball after impact. Many tennis shots can be produced from different strokes, and it is worthwhile learning a few of them in order to improve your game. Using different shots makes for a more enjoyable game as you can use different tactics against your opponent.

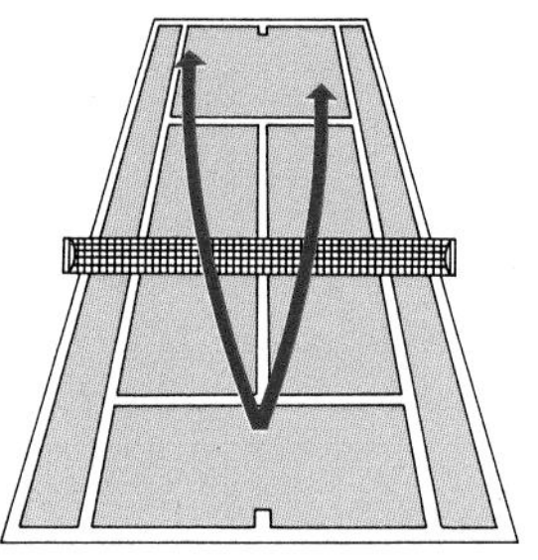

APPROACH SHOT
Play this groundstroke to any part of the court as you approach the net to volley.

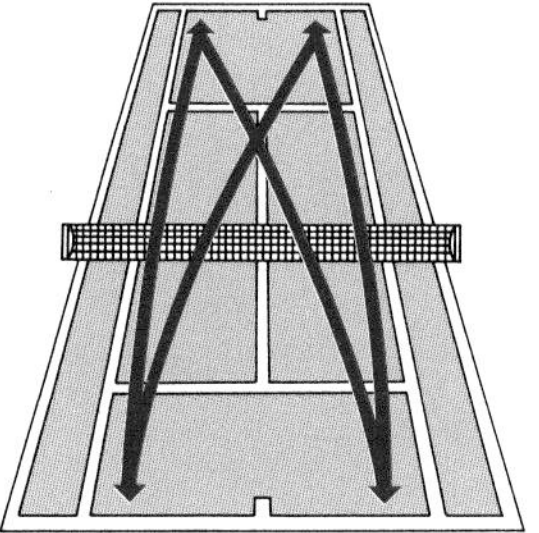

CROSS-COURT & DOWN-THE-LINE
Employ either shot to keep your opponent on the run and pinned in the backcourt.

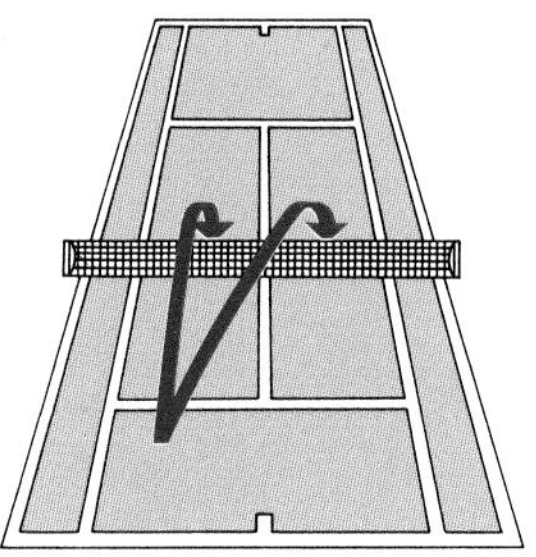

DROP SHOT
Usually underspun, the drop shot should land just over the net with little bounce.

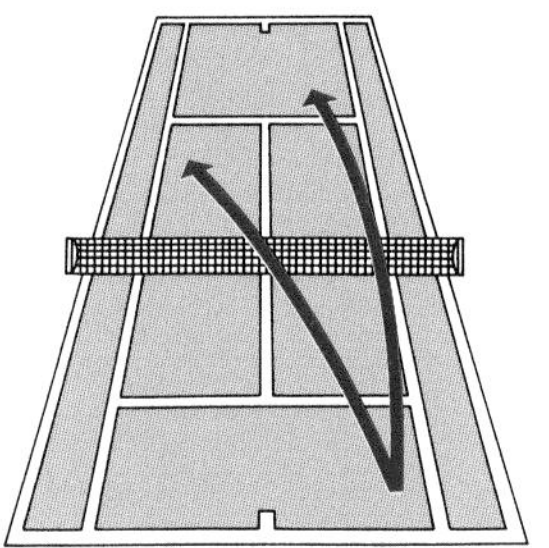

PASSING SHOT
Passing shots don't need depth; just hit them past your advancing opponent.

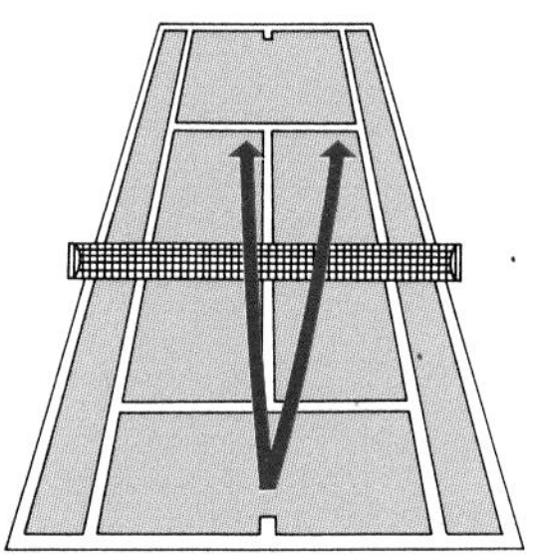

CHIP SHOT
Chip the ball at your opponent's feet or angle it past him as he approaches the net.

THE FOREHAND

24 THE PERFECT FOREHAND

The key to a perfect forehand drive is to develop an aggressive approach from the beginning. If you have an urge to attack the ball on the forehand side, go for it. The forehand is the major groundstroke for both beginner and advanced player alike and is the most natural groundstroke to use. When using the forehand drive, develop a flowing movement that allows you to run for your next shot or recover to your previous position.

After hitting ball, follow its flight with racket face
Begin take-back before reaching hitting area
Turn sideways-on and set off on either foot, adjusting footwork as you go
Position yourself parallel to ball's flight and unwind naturally as you step into the ball
Let back foot swing through after impact, using it to launch yourself off towards next location

THE FLIGHT OF THE BALL
To hit your forehand drive deep to the far baseline, aim another net's height, about 1 m (3 ft), over the net.

25 THE BEST FOREHAND GRIP

How you hold the racket can dictate your method of play. Begin with a natural grip to allow the body to perform smoothly. The most natural grip for the forehand is often the basic Eastern Forehand grip, but three other grips might suit you better. Racket handles have planes and slants, so getting the grip right is easy. Grips affect the position of your feet, so adopt the footwork that complements your choice of grip.

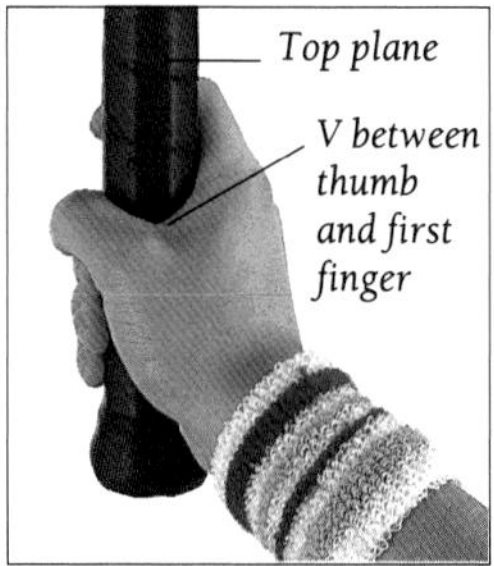

MODIFIED EASTERN GRIP
Place the V between thumb and first finger in the centre of the top plane. Place your palm behind the handle with your thumb wrapped round.

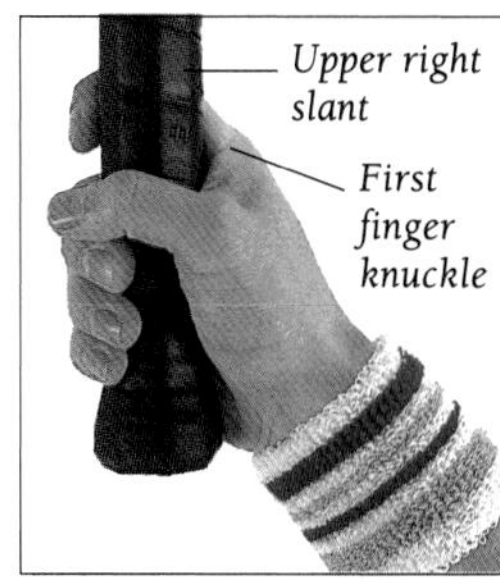

SEMI-WESTERN GRIP
Place your V on the upper right slant of the racket and the knuckle of your first finger on the top edge of the lower right slant.

WESTERN GRIP
Place your V on the rear plane with your first finger knuckle on the lower right slant. The palm is placed towards the bottom plane.

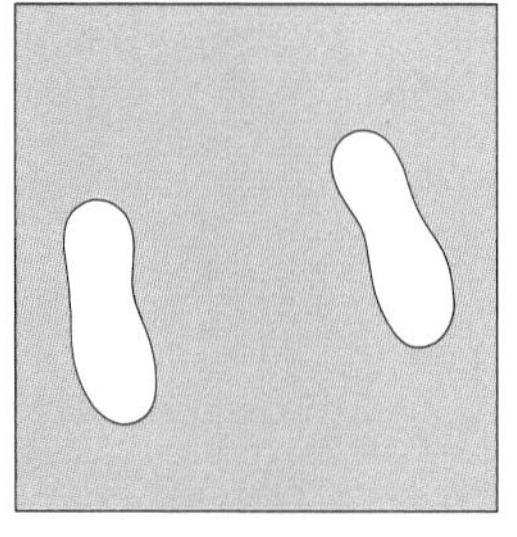

CLOSED STANCE
Turn on your right foot to get sideways-on to the ball. Now step in almost parallel to the ball's flight with your left foot.

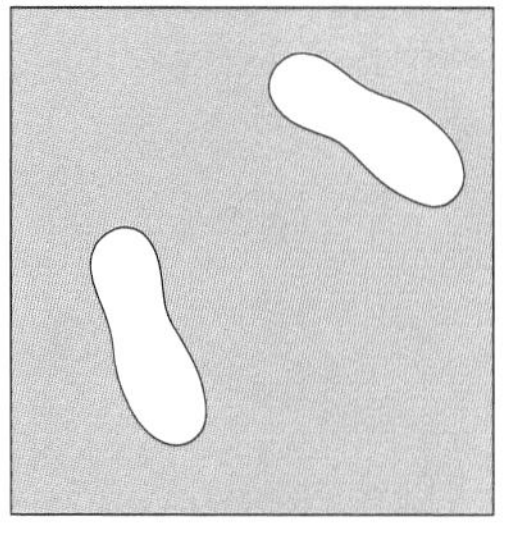

SEMI-OPEN STANCE
Place your back foot more behind than parallel to ball's flight. Step in more openly, releasing the upper body's rotational momentum.

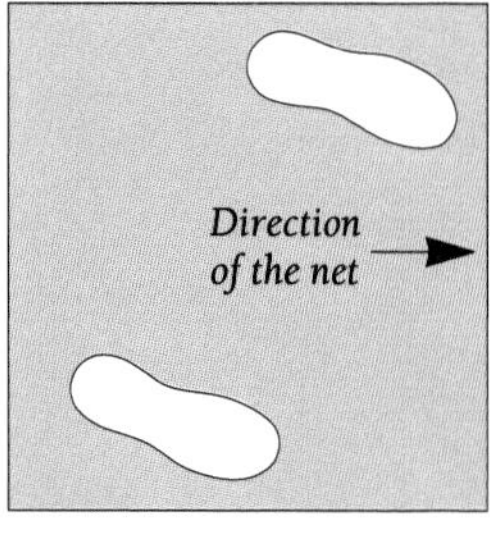

OPEN STANCE
Your back foot positions you and steps in behind the ball simultaneously. Your other foot moves marginally forwards to aid balance.

26 THE TAKE-BACK

To get ready to hit the ball, turn sideways-on from the ready position you have already learned, release your non-playing hand for balance, and flex your knees as you take the racket back early at the hitting height. At the end of your take-back, relax your elbow and let your racket head form a natural loop, adding rhythm and speed to provide a positive feeling of lift to your forward swing.

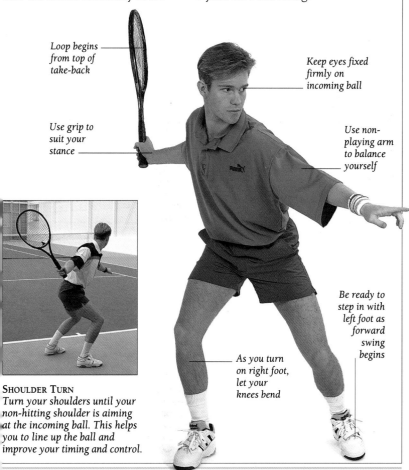

Loop begins from top of take-back

Keep eyes fixed firmly on incoming ball

Use grip to suit your stance

Use non-playing arm to balance yourself

Be ready to step in with left foot as forward swing begins

As you turn on right foot, let your knees bend

SHOULDER TURN
Turn your shoulders until your non-hitting shoulder is aiming at the incoming ball. This helps you to line up the ball and improve your timing and control.

27 THE HIT

To ensure a perfect hit every time, step in with your left foot and swing the racket head up to meet the ball between knee and waist height. Swing the racket head across the hip line from low to high, and extend your arm without locking the elbow. Hitting with a bent elbow means you are too close to the ball and can result in a loss of power and control over your shot.

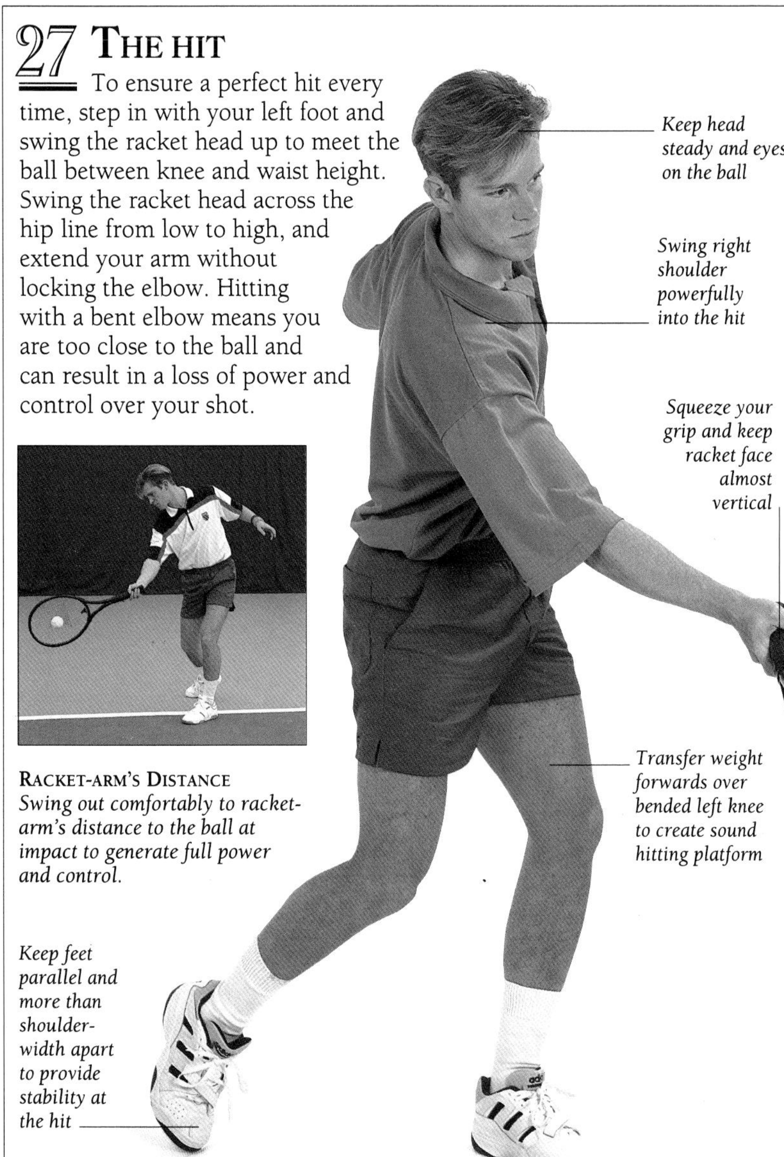
Keep head steady and eyes on the ball
Swing right shoulder powerfully into the hit
Squeeze your grip and keep racket face almost vertical
Transfer weight forwards over bended left knee to create sound hitting platform
Keep feet parallel and more than shoulder-width apart to provide stability at the hit

RACKET-ARM'S DISTANCE
Swing out comfortably to racket-arm's distance to the ball at impact to generate full power and control.

28 The follow-through

Once you have hit the ball, don't stop! You need to carry on to keep up the momentum so you naturally regain the ready position in time for the next shot. So, after hitting the ball, continue swinging your racket head through the hitting zone – the general area of the court where you strike the ball – to above head height with a powerful, lifting action. Keep the racket face steady as it follows the flight of the ball.

Follow-through should be unrestricted and natural
Maintain balance as you shift body weight through hitting zone
Front leg provides sound hitting base
Let right foot stabilize the hit and then swing through to aid natural recovery
Pivot on left foot as you follow through

29 Practising

To improve your forehand, get your partner to drop balls for you to hit over the net. Next, get him to throw balls underarm to you over the net, simulating an opponent's shot, for you to hit back.

- Then rally from mid-court, hitting cross-court drives to each other in the diagonally opposite service area.
- When you can keep a 10-shot rally going, move back until you can rally with each other from behind the baselines. Try a 10-shot rally to begin with, then aim for a 20-shot rally, hitting drives deep into each other's forehand corners and making each ball bounce between the service line and the baseline.
- Be sure to recover to a central position behind the centre mark after each shot, to practise the movements that matchplay requires.

30 ATTACKING PLAY

Attack your opponent by playing forehand drives deep into his or her forehand and backhand corners to pin him in the backcourt. Aim your shots cross-court. When he switches to a down-the-line drive, it will be easier to return the ball in either direction.

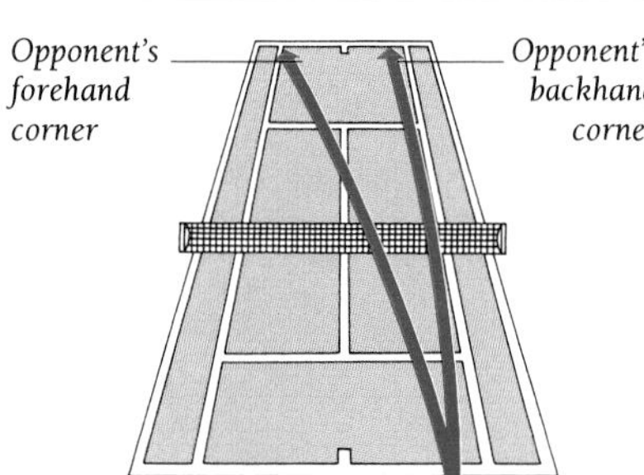

31 ADDING TOPSPIN

Applying topspin to your forehand drive can put your opponent off-guard. It is a useful accessory to your basic forehand attack. Use a full Eastern or a Semi-Western grip. On the take-back, bring the racket back at about the hitting height and form a deep loop with the racket head as you join the take-back to the forward swing.

Keep wrist action freer than for basic drive

Use free hand for balance

Racket strings brush steeply up back of ball to impart severe topspin

Follow throug naturally letting elbow ben

Sweep racket head through hit from low to high

THE TAKE-BACK

THE HIT

THE FOLLOW-THROUGH

THE BACKHAND

32 THE PERFECT BACKHAND

The key to a perfect backhand is the ability to uncoil into the hit with power. Develop also the ability to turn and run while at the same time preparing your stroke and getting in the right position in the hitting area. Add this on-the-move drive to your groundstroke play and gain full control in the backcourt.

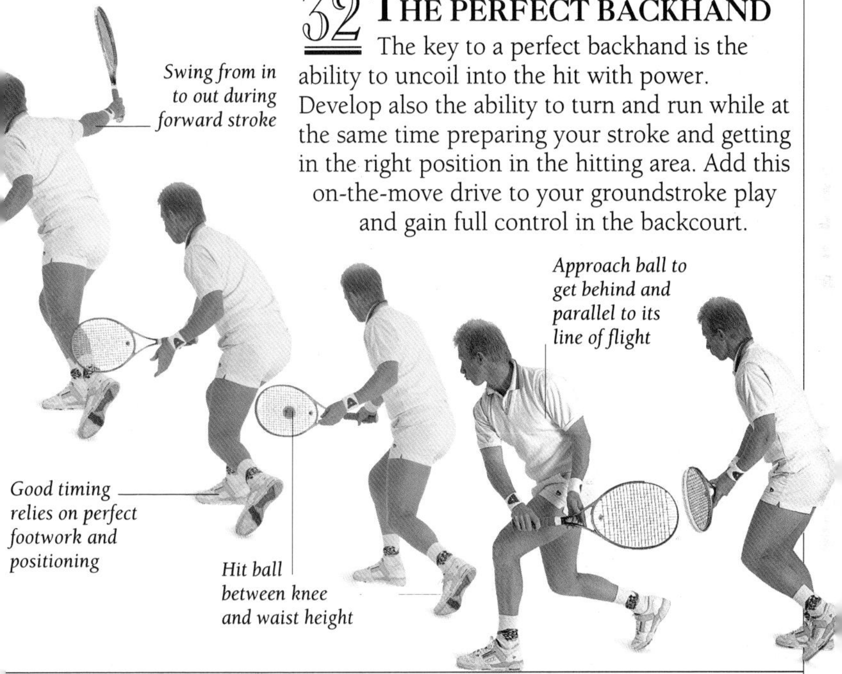

Swing from in to out during forward stroke
Approach ball to get behind and parallel to its line of flight
Good timing relies on perfect footwork and positioning
Hit ball between knee and waist height

33 THE BEST GRIP

Use an Eastern Backhand grip for the backhand drive. For this, you place your V in the upper left slant of the racket handle and your thumb across the rear plane. The knuckle of your first finger is on the upper right slant. Combined with a firm wrist, this grip will help you to develop a powerful, well-controlled backhand drive.

Upper right slant
Rear plane
Upper left slant

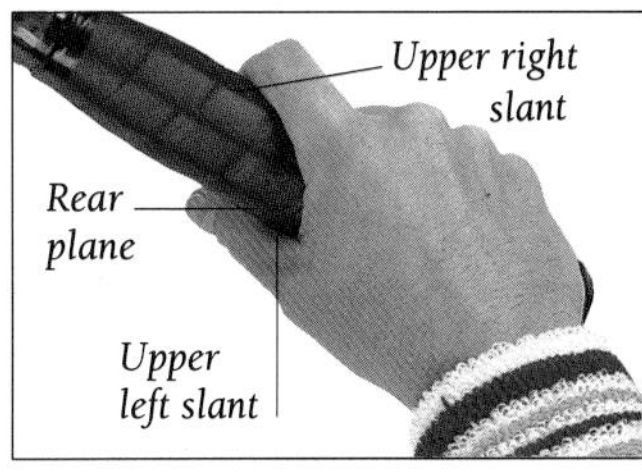

EASTERN BACKHAND GRIP

34 THE TAKE-BACK

From the ready position, face the net from behind your baseline. Hold the racket in front, supporting it with your non-playing hand. Turn your shoulders fully and shift your weight onto your left foot. Keep your support hand on the racket as you bring it behind your left hip. Complete the take-back with your back facing towards the net. Your weight is ready to be transferred forwards as your body uncoils and your right foot steps in.

Take racket right back before beginning loop
Pivot whole body around and try to get hips parallel to flight of ball
Look over hitting shoulder at oncoming ball
Let knee bend as you turn away to play the shot

READY TO HIT
As you turn your shoulders, put your weight on your back foot. Your racket will loop down before swinging up and out.

35 MAKING ROOM TO SWING

It is very important to give yourself plenty of room to swing out and up to meet the ball. Begin the step-in and forward swing at the same time. Joining the back and forward swing with a shallow loop, swing the racket in a broad sweep from low to high, through the hitting zone. Focus on the ball and meet it in front of you.

36 POWERFUL STROKES

The easy power in the backhand comes from the uncoiling action of your body and playing arm. To deliver power with control, pivot on your back foot and turn your hitting shoulder until your back faces the net. With your racket prepared behind your rear hip, you are ready to uncoil with power and accuracy.

37 THE HIT

Release your support hand from the racket, and make a shallow loop with the racket head to ensure a low to high forward swing as you step in. Hit the ball a racket-arm's distance away in the sideways-on position. Your grip will give you a feeling of solidity at impact and provide a natural racket-face angle for lift and direction.

After releasing support hand from racket, extend it for balance

Hold racket arm straight at impact with wrist locked

Keep racket face almost vertical but angled slightly to encourage lift

Transfer body weight onto bent front knee as you sweep racket head up to meet the ball

Step front foot in parallel to ball's line of flight to ensure solid hitting platform

38 The follow-through

To follow through after hitting the ball, feel your racket head lifting through the ball in the direction in which you are aiming. Your racket arm should be straight but not locked out, with your body leaning forwards over your bent front knee. As the follow-through ends, let your back foot swing through and recover to the ready position

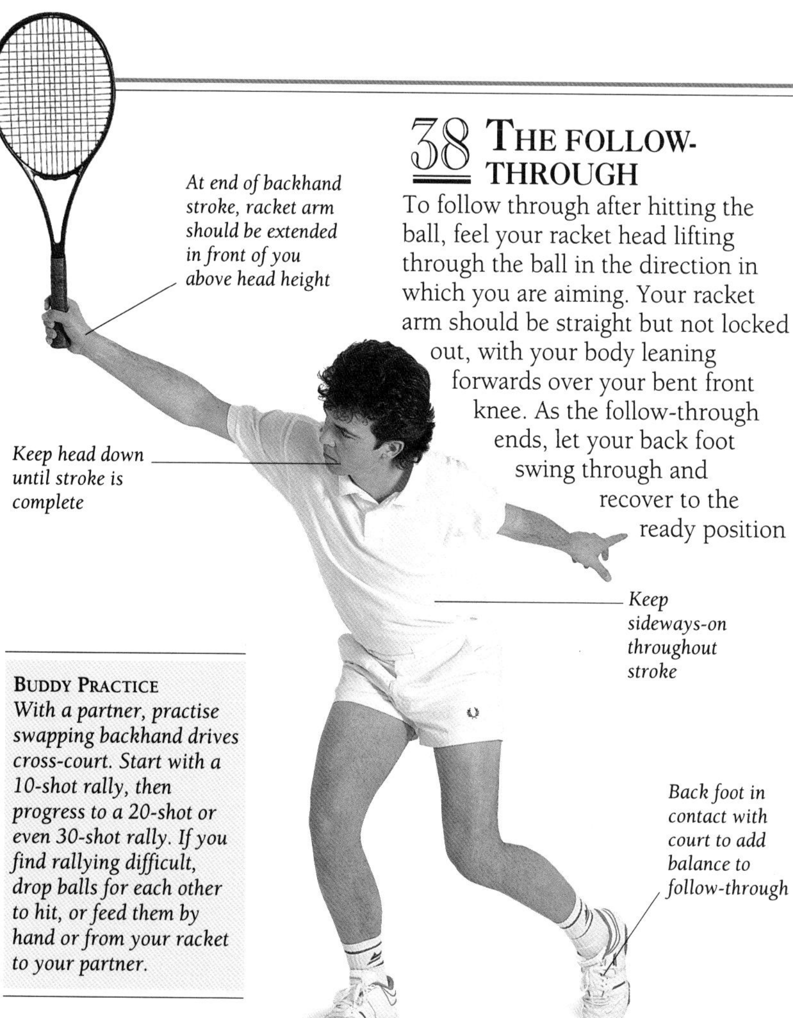

At end of backhand stroke, racket arm should be extended in front of you above head height

Keep head down until stroke is complete

Keep sideways-on throughout stroke

Back foot in contact with court to add balance to follow-through

Buddy Practice
With a partner, practise swapping backhand drives cross-court. Start with a 10-shot rally, then progress to a 20-shot or even 30-shot rally. If you find rallying difficult, drop balls for each other to hit, or feed them by hand or from your racket to your partner.

39 Problem shots

If the ball is coming directly at you, step away from its flight path with your front foot. As you transfer your weight onto this foot, lean away from the ball and fully extend your racket arm at the hit. With a high ball, take your racket back higher than you would for a basic drive. Bring your racket up to meet the ball with the full racket face.

40 BACKHAND DROP

The backhand drop shot is an advanced touch stroke and requires diligent practice. Take your racket back to about head height, with the racket face angled back slightly to allow underspin to be applied. Push the racket head down and under the ball and feel the strings gripping the ball. The ball is deflected up and off the strings, dropping over the net with little bounce as the spin takes its effect. The follow-through is short.

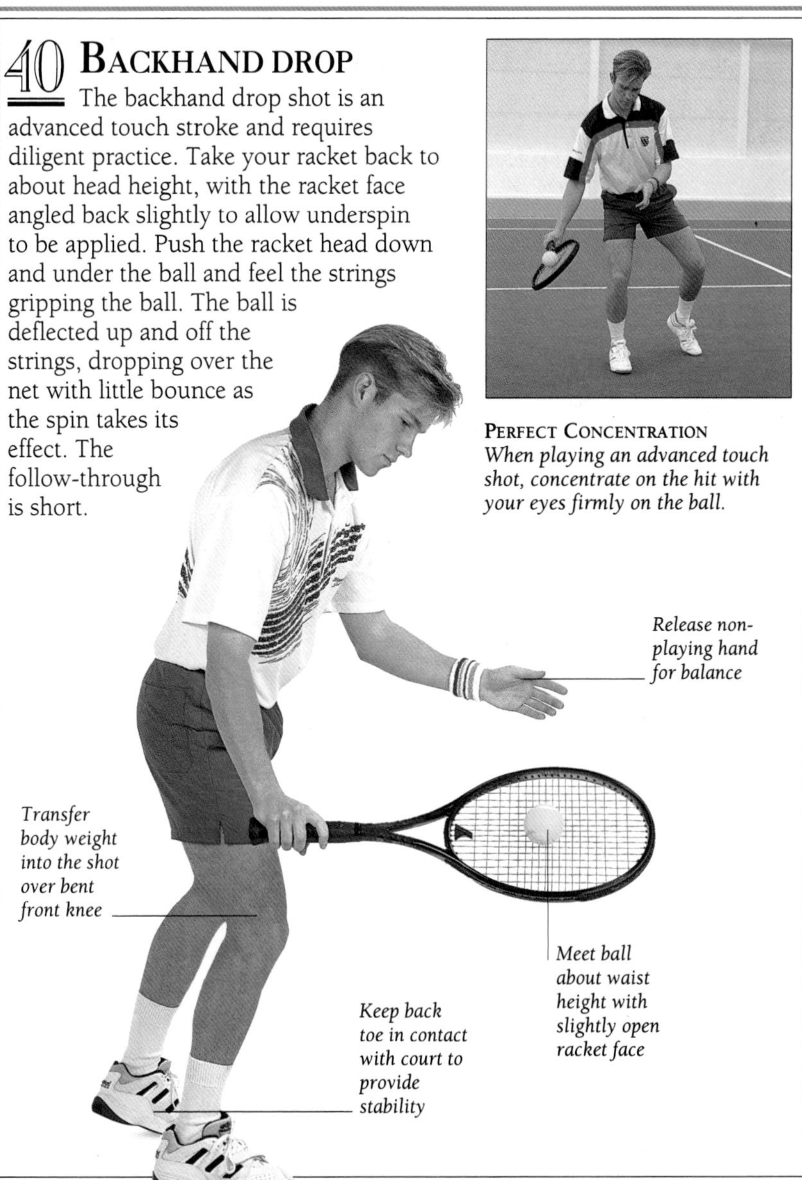

PERFECT CONCENTRATION
When playing an advanced touch shot, concentrate on the hit with your eyes firmly on the ball.

Release non-playing hand for balance

Transfer body weight into the shot over bent front knee

Meet ball about waist height with slightly open racket face

Keep back toe in contact with court to provide stability

41 DOUBLE-HANDED BACKHAND

The double-handed backhand is a perfect option for young players who lack physical strength, and for older players just starting out. This powerful, two-handed stroke will encourage you to attack the ball with topspin and provides a feeling of greater strength and control. When gripping the racket, just add the other hand to begin with, but later on try changing your grip as you begin the take-back.

Point racket head downwards

Let racket sweep out and up through ball

1 As you pivot, ready to hit the ball, simply add your other hand to the handle and take your racket back below your intended hitting height.

Use your back foot for balance

2 Step in with your right foot, swinging your racket to meet the ball in front of your leading hip. Your body weight has shifted onto your front foot.

Finish high for good topspin effect

Whip racket head up with pronounced wrist action to get more topspin on ball

Weight fully transferred as legs and body straighten

3 Allow your body to uncoil fully as you drive through the ball. A firm-wristed drive with a flatter follow-through may provide more pace but less margin for error.

42 CHANGING GRIP

As your double-hander improves, position your playing hand with an Eastern Backhand or Continental grip. Support the racket with your spare hand and turn your playing hand inwards. Slide your support hand down to form a left-handed EasternForehand grip above your right hand.

GRIP CHANGE
Turn playing hand until V between thumb and first finger is on inner edge of handle.

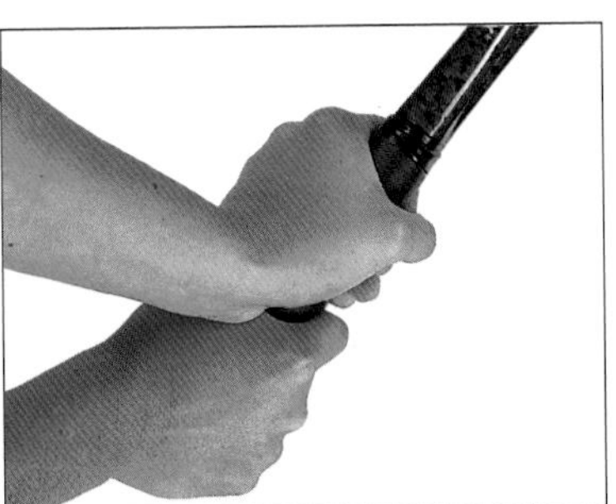

GRIP READY
Slide supporting hand down the handle until it nestles in the V of playing hand.

THE SERVICE

43 THE PERFECT SERVICE

The service is the most devastating stroke in tennis. From a static position, a well-timed service will fire a ball into your opponent's court with deadly precision. For a perfect service, you should feel momentum rising up through your body as your legs, hips, back, shoulders, playing arm, and wrist create a powerful chain reaction.

Stand with feet a good distance apart and knees slightly flexed

To prepare for the serve, push down into the court with back foot

Build power into your service by using your leg muscles

Follow through your service to give yourself momentum for next shot

THE FLIGHT OF THE BALL
The ball travels in an arc from the baseline into the service court diagonally opposite. It reaches the far baseline after the bounce.

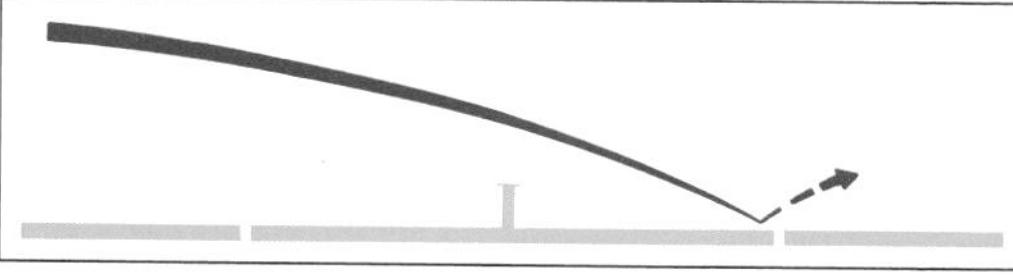

44 GRIPPING THE BALL

To hold one ball, grasp it with the thumb and four fingers of your non-playing hand. To hold two, grip the first ball with your thumb and first two fingers, and the second with your third and fourth fingers.

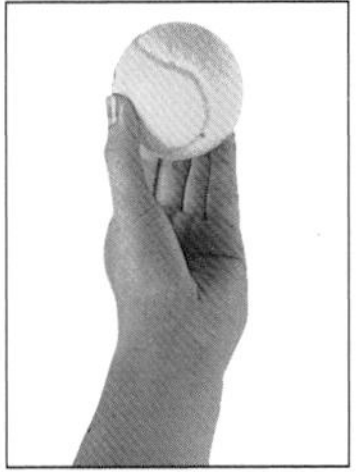

ONE-BALL GRIP

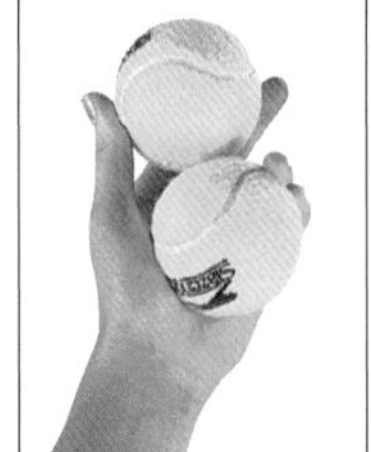

TWO-BALL GRIP

45 THE BEST GRIP

When you first serve, try the Eastern or Modified Eastern forehand grip. Graduate to the Continental grip, where the V between thumb and first finger is to the left of the top plane's centre, with the first finger knuckle on the upper right slant.

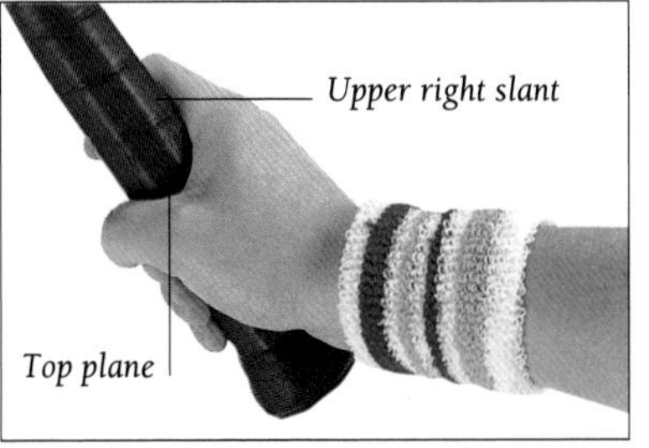
Upper right slant
Top plane

THE CONTINENTAL GRIP

46 SERVING PRACTICE

The service action is simply an overarm throw. If you can throw a ball overarm, you can serve. With a partner at the far baseline, take turns at throwing a ball over the net to each other.

Make ball bounce in diagonally opposite service court
Having bent elbow, extend arm and release ball
Use left arm for balance
Look up and follow ball's flight
Stand behind baseline on either side of centre mark

47 FOOTFAULTS

There is no point in making a perfect service if, before striking the ball, you step onto or over the baseline with either foot. Your service would be disallowed and you could not take it again. To avoid footfaults, have a wider stance and practise keeping your back foot on the ground for several serves.

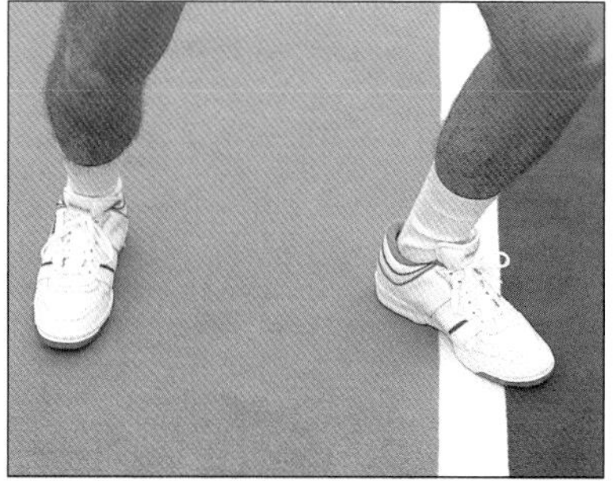

FRONT FOOTFAULT
To cure the above footfault, start with your feet further apart.

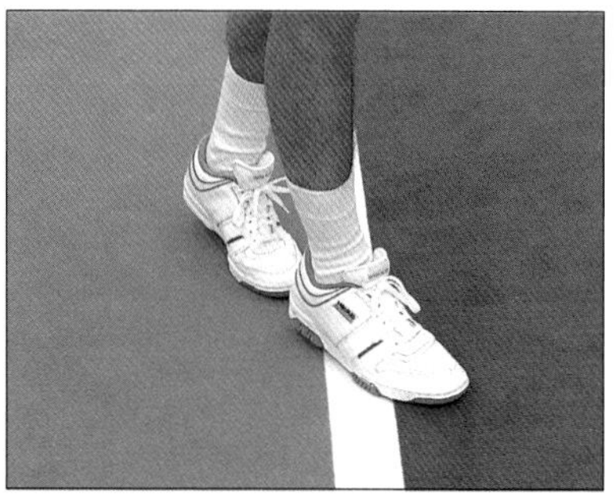

REAR FOOTFAULT
If you throw the ball too far forwards, your back foot may swing across the line too soon.

48 THE SERVICE STANCE

To prepare to serve, stand behind the baseline within 50 cm (1 ft 8 in) of the centre mark. Face your opponent sideways-on to the net with your feet shoulder-width apart. Slightly flex your knees with your weight poised on your back foot. Point your left toe towards the right-hand net post. Put your weight on your rear foot, ready to be transferred forwards as your arms part. Relax your arms and shoulders.

Study your opponent's position, then focus on ball as you begin to serve
Hold balls against racket strings and point racket towards service court
Push into ground with back foot to get your serve in motion

49 THE PLACE-UP

Place the ball up in front of you and a little to your right. As you transfer your weight, use your back foot for stability. When you release the ball, bend your racket arm and lift your racket until the tip points skywards. At the end of the place-up, both arms should point upwards.

Point racket head and placing hand up as ball reaches its peak
Flex front knee to cushion forward movement of your weight

50 THE THROWING POSITION

From the throwing position, don't stop, but feel a pause at the height of the take-up. Then let your racket drop smoothly down into the throwing position, deep between your shoulder blades. Use your trailing leg to stabilize yourself.

Relax elbow to let racket head drop into throwing position, keeping racket clear of body
Maintain balance over bent knee prior to hit

51 THE HIT

To hit the ball over the net perfectly each time, straighten your legs and launch the racket head up. Your body should be fully stretched out at impact, with just your toes on the ground. Extend your racket arm straight up from the shoulder.

Hit ball in middle of strings

Turn hitting shoulder in powerfully as you throw racket head up to meet the ball

Straighten legs at the hit, with back foot no longer anchored, and ready for follow-through action

After impact, place-up arm drops away as follow-through begins

A FEEL FOR THE BALL
In order to improve your accuracy and margin for error over the net, try to develop the feeling that you are hitting up, through, and over the ball.

52 THE FOLLOW-THROUGH

After impact, allow your racket to swing down past your left leg in a full follow-through. At the same time, let your right foot swing across the baseline for balance. Finish with your weight on your right foot and with the right knee bent to assist your recovery behind the baseline or your journey forwards to volley.

Let racket swing past your left side
Keep your eye on the ball as you follow through

53 SLICE SERVICE

The slice service is the cutting edge of your service firepower. Use a slice delivery to swerve the ball sharply through the air before and after the bounce, keeping the ball low as it takes your opponent out of the court. Sidespin makes it safe, so use this alternative technique for your second serve.

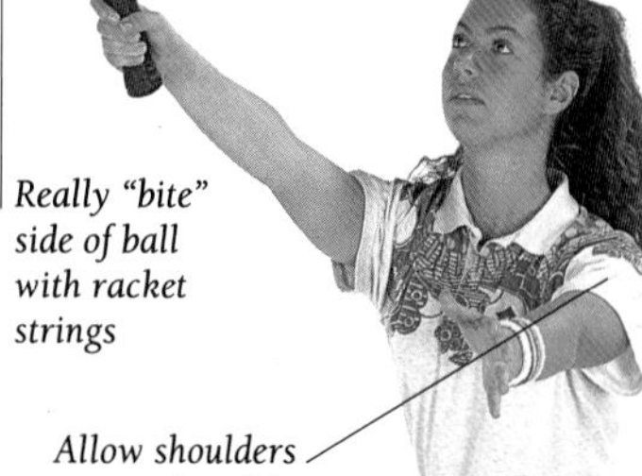
Really "bite" side of ball with racket strings
Allow shoulders to turn in at hit

PLAYING WITH SLICE
In order to perfect the slice service, try to feel your racket cutting across the right side of the ball at 3 o'clock. Always keep your head steady and eyes focused on the ball.

54 DEVELOPING YOUR SERVICE

To maintain tactical advantage in a game, you should aim to get at least 70 per cent of your first service shots into court. To achieve this, practise serving at three-quarters' speed, not flat out. When you can serve either wide, straight at the body, or down the centre against either right- or left-handed players with equal consistency, you will be good enough to win most of your service games. Aim your serves deep or angle them towards the sidelines.

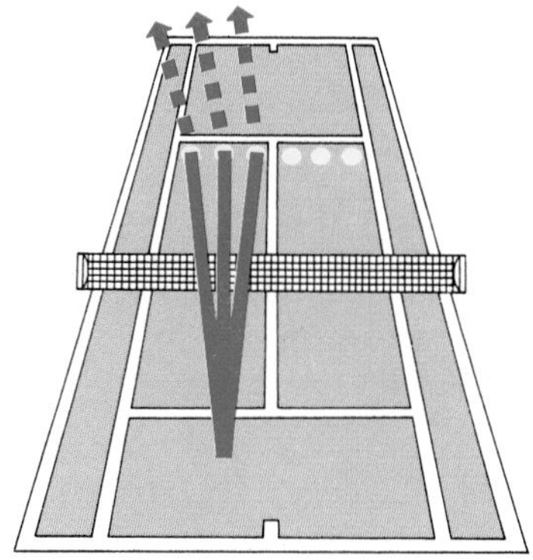

SERVING AT TARGETS
One simple way to develop your serve is to practise serving at targets. Position three targets in your opponent's two serving courts and then serve two balls at each target. Keep a note of how many serves go in to the court as well as counting how many times you hit a target. As your practice scores increase, so should your matchplay serving improve.

SERVICE RETURN

55 THE IMPORTANCE OF THE RETURN

Your ability to return your opponent's serve consistently affects the outcome of every point, and is second only to service in matchplay importance. It is vital to return every service effectively, but the serving strengths of your opponent govern the type and quality of your reply. Learn to adapt your basic forehand and backhand strokes to counteract the height, speed, spin, and placement of the service.

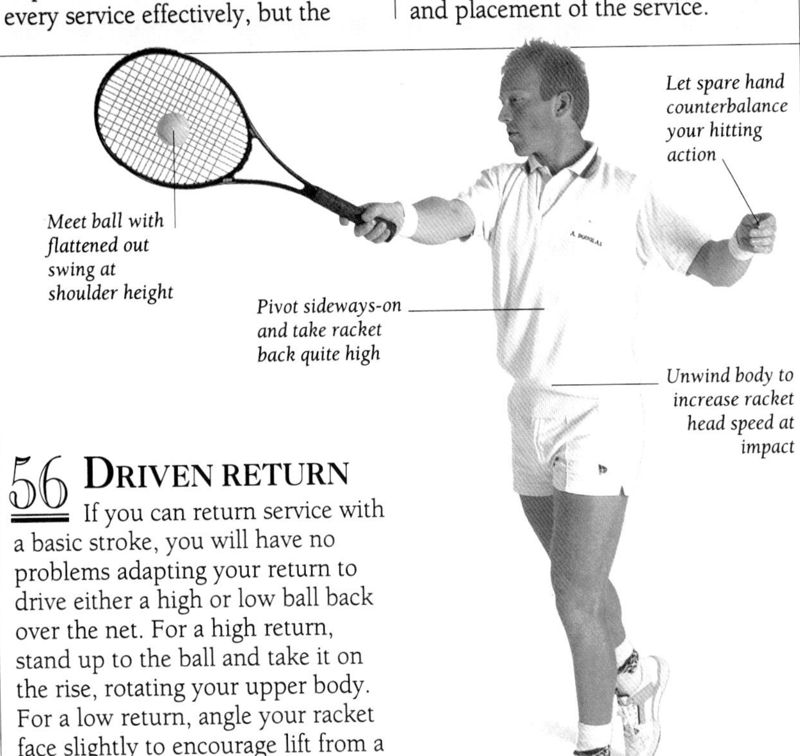
Let spare hand counterbalance your hitting action
Meet ball with flattened out swing at shoulder height
Pivot sideways-on and take racket back quite high
Unwind body to increase racket head speed at impact

56 DRIVEN RETURN

If you can return service with a basic stroke, you will have no problems adapting your return to drive either a high or low ball back over the net. For a high return, stand up to the ball and take it on the rise, rotating your upper body. For a low return, angle your racket face slightly to encourage lift from a bent-knee position.

57 BLOCKED RETURN

A blocked return is played with a short take-back and a volley-like punch. Stand just inside your baseline and take the ball early. Block or punch through the back of the ball and aim deep to the far baseline to cancel out the server's advantage.

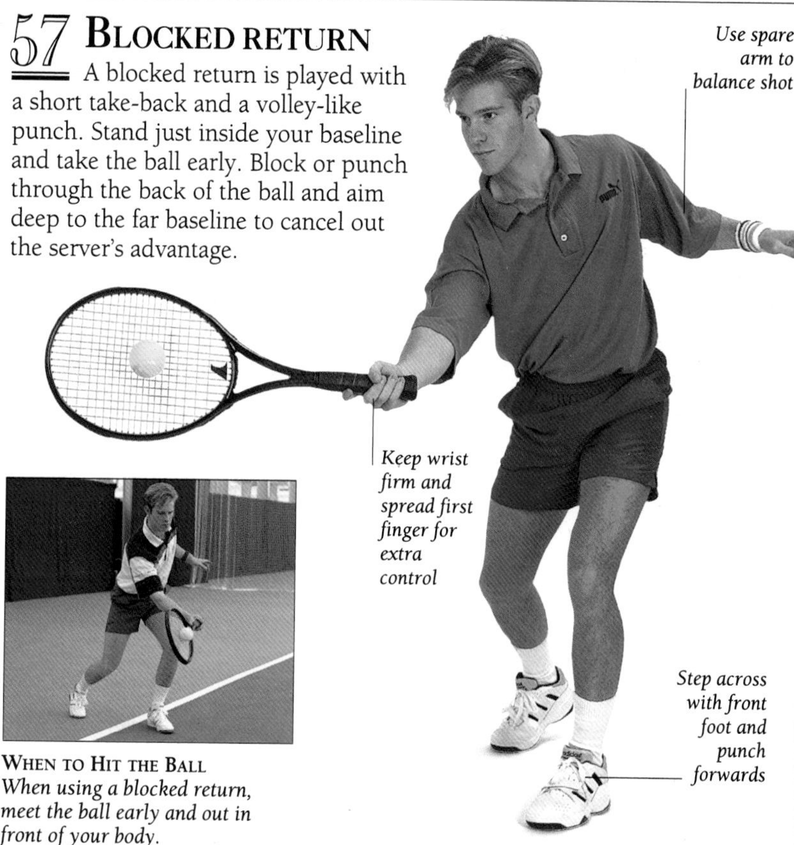
Use spare arm to balance shot
Keep wrist firm and spread first finger for extra control
Step across with front foot and punch forwards

WHEN TO HIT THE BALL
When using a blocked return, meet the ball early and out in front of your body.

58 ATTACKING & SURPRISE RETURNS

To respond to a short-length service, take the ball early and hit it down the sideline or cross-court. The server is unlikely to approach the net behind such a serve, so your attacking return should put him on the defensive and allow you to move up-court. If the serve is even shorter, angle your return for a winner.

If the server aims deep to your backhand, respond with a topspin lobbed return cross-court or down-the-line. It will catch him flatfooted as he moves in.

59 LOBBED RETURN

For a lobbed return, move forwards inside your baseline and form a short, low take-back before stepping in to sweep your racket head up the back of the ball to give it heavy topspin. Use your basic Eastern Backhand grip for this shot, playing the return with a firm wrist.

WHEN TO HIT THE BALL
Take a high, bouncing serve on the rise, meeting the ball at about shoulder height.

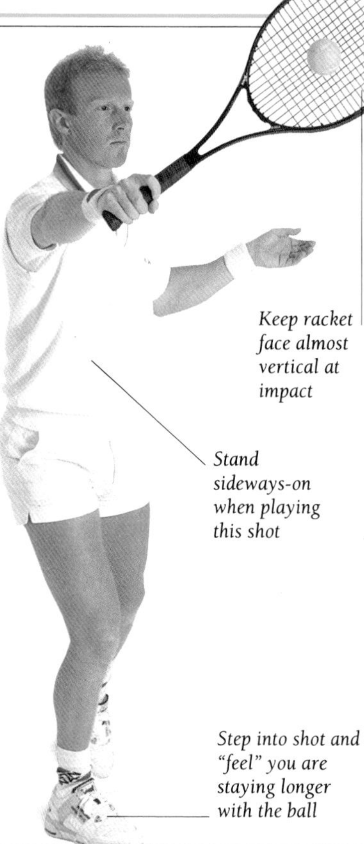

Keep racket face almost vertical at impact
Stand sideways-on when playing this shot
Step into shot and "feel" you are staying longer with the ball

60 RETURN TACTICS

When a service is delivered down-the-line to your backhand from the right court, move forwards inside your baseline and chip your return low at the feet of your opponent. Alternatively, aim towards the sidelines to draw him or her wide and open up the court for you to play a passing shot.

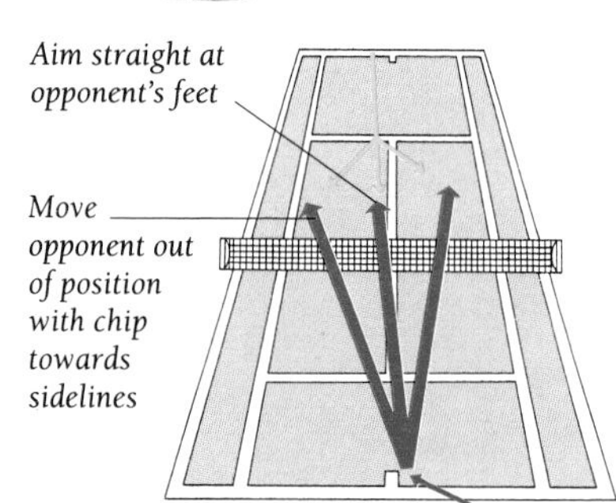

61 CHIPPED RETURN

The chipped return is a short, underspun stroke very useful against spinning or high, bouncing serves. To play this return, move inside your baseline and make a short, high take-back, chipping down through the ball between waist and shoulder height. Keep your racket with the ball after contact. The ideal chipped return is played wide of, or at the feet of, an incoming volleyer, landing in the opposite service court areas.

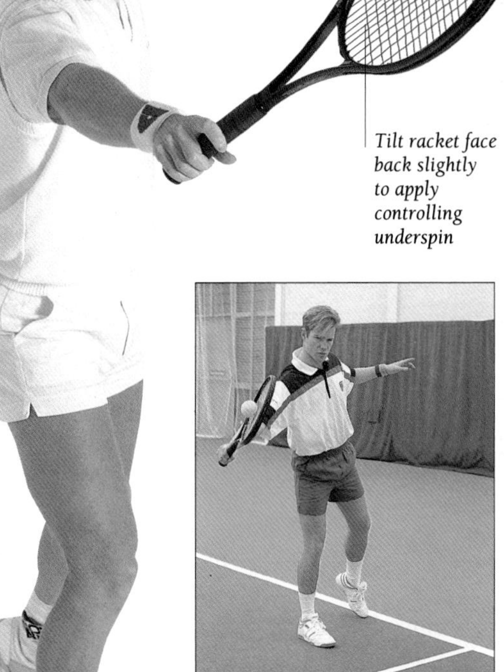

Keep your eyes focused on the ball at impact

Tilt racket face back slightly to apply controlling underspin

Keep feet parallel to or slightly across line of flight of ball

WHEN TO HIT THE BALL
It is important to meet the ball well in front of your body, with your racket arm extended, when playing a chipped return.

CHIP AND CHARGE
A good alternative use for the chipped return is to use it as an offensive weapon, by chipping the ball deep towards your opponent's baseline and then following it in yourself to the net to catch your opponent off-guard.

THE FOREHAND VOLLEY

62 THE PERFECT FOREHAND VOLLEY

The forehand volley is one of the most decisive shots in tennis, and can be the match-winning shot in your game. Play the volley like a boxer's jabbing punch. Advance towards the net and jab your racket head forwards to hit the ball before it bounces. The volley is a short, punched stroke that travels from high to low, compared to the low-to-high swing of the equivalent groundstroke.

Resist temptation to take a swing at the ball when volleying on the move
Always carry racket in front of you, ready for instant action
Split-step in order to anticipate height and direction of incoming ball
Keep take-back short for control and play forwards for pace

THE FLIGHT OF THE BALL
In a volley, the ball has only one flight. Try to meet it above net height and aim straight into your opponent's court.

63 POSITIONING HANDS & FEET

To begin with, you will feel more confident using the basic Eastern Forehand grip. Place your palm behind the handle and simply "shake hands" with the racket. As you improve, graduate to the Continental grip you learned for service for greater flexibility. Spread your first finger more to give you an increased feel for the ball.

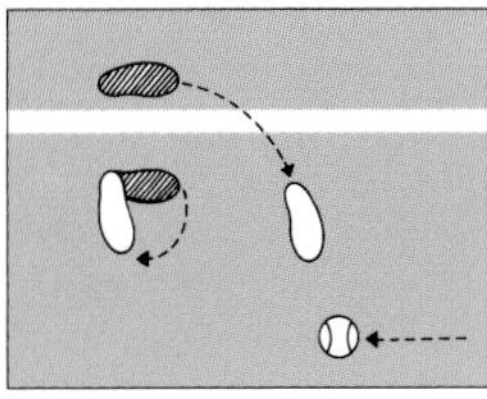

EASY BALL
To return an easy ball, turn on your right foot and step forwards with your left foot, parallel to ball's flight line.

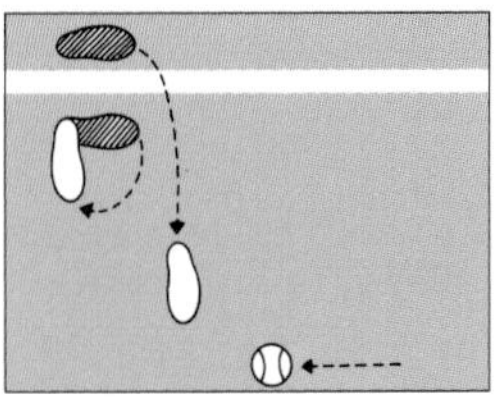

WIDE BALL
To hit a wide ball, pivot to your right and step well across with left foot. Rotate upper body for balance.

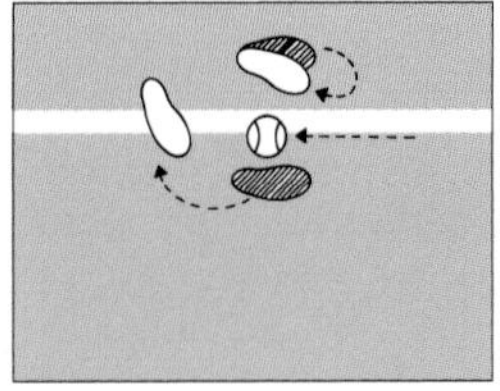

BODYLINE BALL
Pivot on left foot and then step back with your right to get sideways-on before leaning weight forwards.

64 GRABBING THE BALL

The forehand volley action is just like catching the ball with your playing hand, and you can improve your forehand volley with this simple exercise. Stand on the opposite side of the net to your partner, about 3 m (10 ft) back. Ask your partner to throw you a ball underarm at shoulder height. Reach forwards and firmly grab the ball to the side and in front of you before it starts to fall towards the ground. Focus on the ball and "stop" it with your eyes as you make the grab. Now throw the ball back for your partner to grab.

Always use spare hand to counterbalance your movements

Step forwards and across as you reach out to grab ball, stabilizing movement with back foot

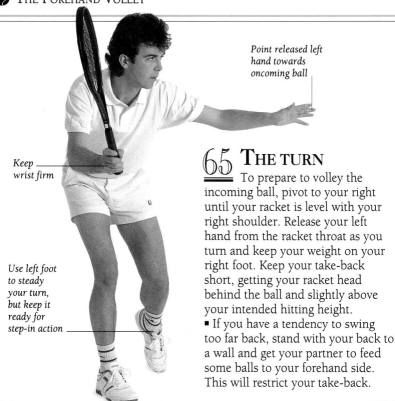

Point released left hand towards oncoming ball

Keep wrist firm

Use left foot to steady your turn, but keep it ready for step-in action

65 THE TURN

To prepare to volley the incoming ball, pivot to your right until your racket is level with your right shoulder. Release your left hand from the racket throat as you turn and keep your weight on your right foot. Keep your take-back short, getting your racket head behind the ball and slightly above your intended hitting height.

▪ If you have a tendency to swing too far back, stand with your back to a wall and get your partner to feed some balls to your forehand side. This will restrict your take-back.

66 VOLLEYER TO VOLLEYER

Develop the accuracy and control of your volley by regularly practising with a partner. Stand on either side of the net in your respective volley positions. Take it in turns to feed balls to each other at increasing speeds, progressing to a volley rally. Keep the emphasis on fast footwork when turning and stepping in, quick reactions, and minimum take-back.

VOLLEY FOR GOALS
Compete with your partner by volleying between two footballs to score goals.

67 THE HIT

When playing a volley, punch your racket head forwards to meet the ball in front of your body between waist and shoulder height. Try to play the ball at eye level.

- Develop the accuracy and control of your forehand volley by aiming at a target on a wall. Try to keep a 10-shot or 20-shot rally going.

GRAB-PUNCH POSITION
Meet the ball higher and closer to your body than you would in groundstroke play.

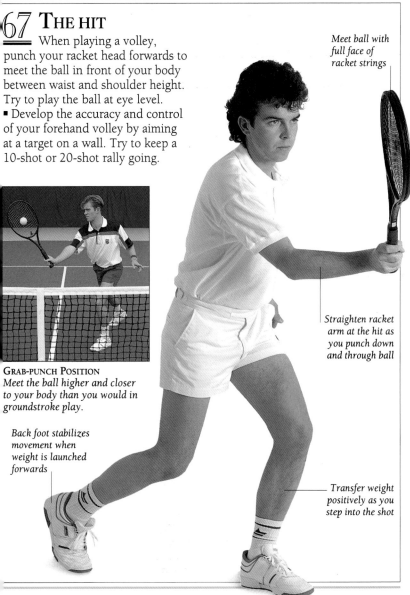

Meet ball with full face of racket strings

Straighten racket arm at the hit as you punch down and through ball

Back foot stabilizes movement when weight is launched forwards

Transfer weight positively as you step into the shot

68 THE FOLLOW-THROUGH

After impact, let your shoulder power through as you complete the shot. Keep your knees bent to maintain good stability and a low centre of gravity. The slight downward path of your racket adds underspin for shot control. Keep the follow-through short.

▪ From a sound net position, volley deep down the sideline to pin your opponent in the backcourt, or try an angled cross-court volley to place the ball out of reach.

Keep head steady and eyes focused on ball

With your elbow well away from body, keep racket arm straight and racket head at about wrist level

After completing stroke, let back foot swing through to aid recovery

Maintain solid hitting platform in follow-through

69 LOW FOREHAND VOLLEY

To play a low volley well, crouch down and bend your knees. Keep your wrist firm and your racket head level. Move into your volley by stepping forwards and across with your front foot.

Use free hand for balance

Angle racket face slightly to apply some underspin

70 HIGH FOREHAND VOLLEY

.n order to play a good, high 'orehand volley, you must position yourself sideways-on, otherwise you nay pull the ball down into the net or play it wide of the sidelines. Take he racket a little further back and nigher than for the basic volley. Then step in with your left foot, punching the racket head down and hrough the ball. Follow through with the racket head in the direction of the shot.

High volleys need strong arms to punch the ball powerfully at shoulder height, so a good level of fitness is required for this shot.

Use free arm for balance
Keep wrist firm and racket head up
Keep both feet on ground

71 FOREHAND HALF-VOLLEY

A half-volley is an advanced stroke played immediately after the ball has bounced. The take-back must be short and low, with the racket head at wrist level. Let your knees bend as you turn on your rear foot and get down low with your front foot forwards and your back knee close to the ground. Meet the ball just after the bounce, keeping your wrist firm.

Use left hand for balance
Get wrist and racket head in line

THE BACKHAND VOLLEY

72 THE PERFECT BACKHAND VOLLEY

You may find that the backhand volley is easier to play than its forehand counterpart, because when you take up the sideways-on position, your playing arm leads the way and encourages positive action. Develop both your backhand and forehand volley sequences by starting from further back and then moving in quickly to volley.

Always have racket ready to make your forward play

Keep your eyes on ball all the way through shot

Release non-playing hand as you punch racket head down through back of ball

Keep feet well apart and body well balanced

THE FLIGHT OF THE BALL
As in the forehand volley, the ball has only one flight. Meet it above net height and aim into opponent's court.

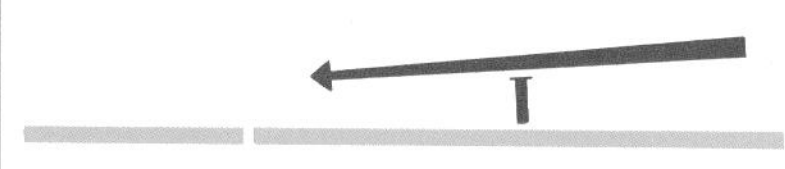

73 THE TURN

Turn sideways-on to the ball from your ready position and take your racket back above hitting height about level with your left shoulder. Support the racket at the throat with your non-playing hand. Flex your knees slightly, with your back foot forming a firm base for hitting. For low balls, bend your knees more.

Keep wrist firm in Eastern Backhand grip
Weight poised on back leg will be transferred to front foot at the hit

74 THE HIT

Releasing your left hand, step forwards and across slightly with your right foot. Punch your racket head forwards and down through the back of the ball, meeting it between waist and shoulder height with the full face of your racket strings. As you hit the ball, transfer your weight fully over your bent front knee. Try to keep your feet parallel to, or slightly across, the line of the ball's flight.

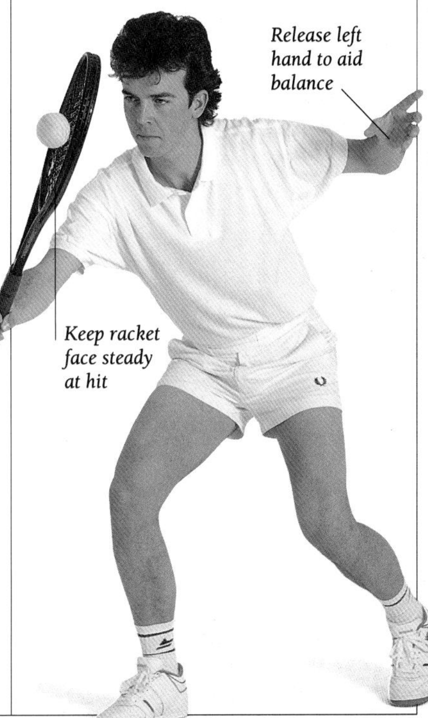

75 THE FOLLOW-THROUGH

Let your racket head follow through a short distance to finish the hitting zone, extending your racket arm as you play right through the ball. The slightly downward action of the racket, with its bottom edge leading, will apply some underspin to the ball for added control. Control your step-in to stay with the ball in the follow-through.

Keep your eyes focused firmly on ball
Left hand out for balance
Extend playing arm with wrist locked and keep racket face steady
Lean whole body forwards as you play through the ball
Keep feet apart to aid stability and lower your centre of gravity

SHOULDER TURN
Avoid getting caught square-on at the net and so dragging the ball down. Get your hitting shoulder well round towards the net as you pivot sideways-on to the oncoming ball.

76 WALL WORK

Volley against a practice wall to improve your stroke. Stand 2 m (6 ft) away: this shortens your stroke and improves your racket-head control. Start from a sideways-on position, returning to your ready position between each volley. Keep a 10- or 20-shot rally going to begin with and then aim for a target on the wall to develop greater accuracy.

77 VOLLEY TACTICS

Volley the ball deep into the corners of your opponent's court, especially from the mid-court area. When you move in closer there will be opportunities to play angled volleys. Aim to volley straight most of the time, remembering that when you do volley cross-court, you must be decisive as it opens up a down-the-line shot for your opponent.

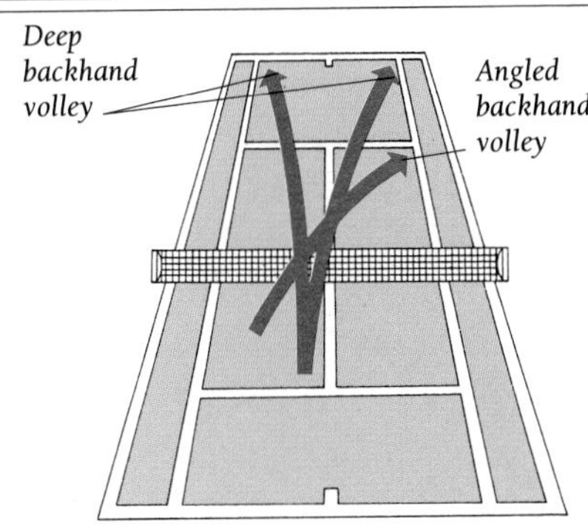

78 BACKHAND HALF-VOLLEY

Like its forehand counterpart, the backhand half-volley is an advanced touch stroke and needs delicate timing. Play your half-volley about mid-court if your approach to the net is too slow. Bend your knees as you turn to make the shot, and step in to play forwards from a short take-back. Meet the ball just after the bounce with a lifting motion.

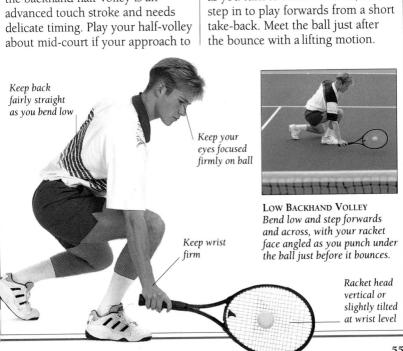

Keep back fairly straight as you bend low

Keep your eyes focused firmly on ball

Keep wrist firm

Racket head vertical or slightly tilted at wrist level

LOW BACKHAND VOLLEY *Bend low and step forwards and across, with your racket face angled as you punch under the ball just before it bounces.*

Lob & Smash

79 The perfect lob

A lob is a ball sent high in the air. It requires a fuller stroke than the drive, with a lower take-back and higher finish. It is not just a defensive stroke, for if you have enough speed to the ball, combined with good racket control at impact, your perfectly measured lob can turn defence into attack.

Move off diagonally to intercept ball shortly after bounce

Racket face angled back for underspin

To hit ball with underspin, hold racket with a short, high take-back

Use basic Eastern Backhand or Continental grip for this advanced backhand lob

Get right down to make shot, with legs wide apart and a low centre of gravity

The Flight of the Ball
The basic lob carries a little topspin and should travel in an even arc, clearing the net by about 7 m (22 ft) to land just inside the opposite baseline. The second flight after the bounce should be fairly high.

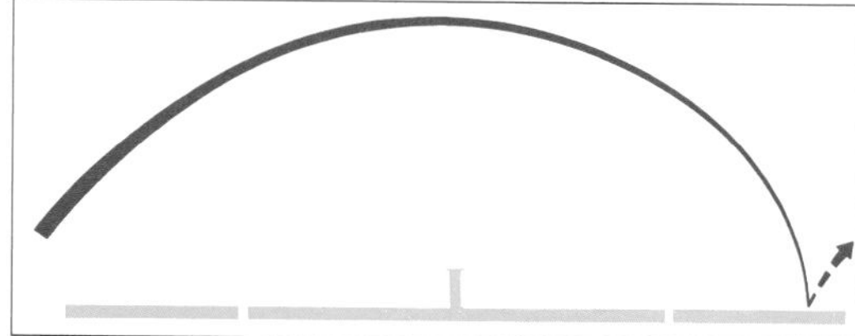

80 The take-back

Begin your basic lob like a drive, taking your racket back as you turn sideways-on. Relax your elbow at the end of the take-back, letting your racket form a low loop. Step in and start to swing the racket head forwards in a steep upwards path.

Point left hand towards ball to help you balance

Use Eastern Forehand grip and keep racket face open

Step in onto flexed front knee as you begin the forward swing from the take-back

When to Lob
The lob can be a good attacking stroke. Drop a lob behind your opponent and close in as he scampers back to base on the defence, or use one early in the rally to play havoc with his confidence.

81 Lob tactics

Generally, lob deep as short lobs are snapped up by net players. Lob over your opponent's non-playing shoulder to his backhand corner because a smash is difficult to play if you have to move diagonally backwards to reach the ball. Play the basic backhand lob with a degree of topspin to make the ball bounce away from your opponent.

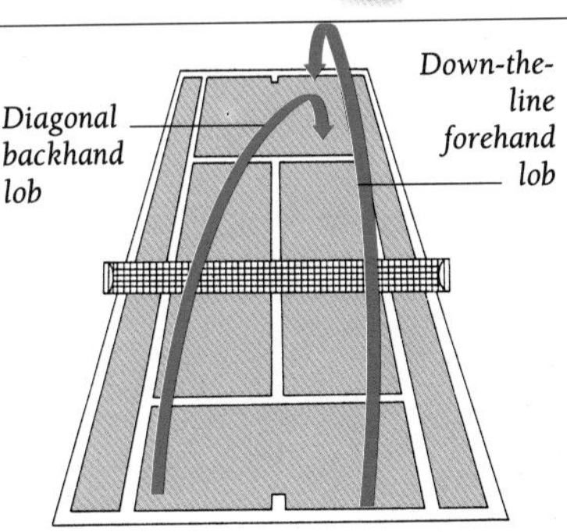

82 The hit

Leading with the bottom edge of your racket face, let the racket swing forwards in a steep, upwards path to meet the ball in front of your leading hip. Squeeze your grip at impact to steady your wrist, and time your swing to meet the ball between knee and waist height as it falls. You can lob off either foot and vary the height and depth of your lob if your hitting platform is sound.

High Follow-through
After impact, let your racket swing up through the hitting zone to finish above your head.

Keep head steady and eyes on ball

Bring left hand back to act as stabilizer as you turn into the hit

Keep racket face angled back for lift, but not too much or lob will fall short

Bent knee aiding lift will straighten as follow-through develops

83 THE PERFECT SMASH

The jump smash epitomizes on-the-move action; it overcomes any lack of reach you might have and deals effectively with deep lobs. To play the shot well, develop speed and agility to move backwards in a sideways-on position, and power in your legs for leaping high in the air. Use the side-step or cross-over for your run back.

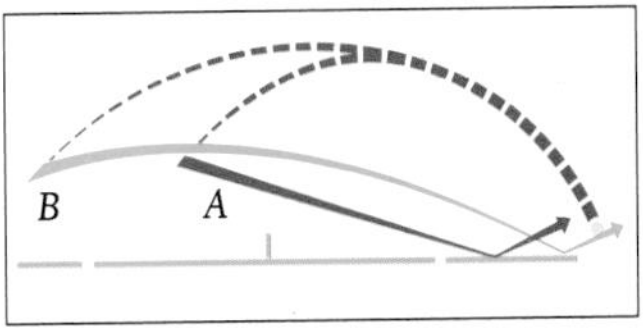

THE FLIGHT OF THE BALL
From close in at the net (A), angle your smash to make it bounce over your opponent's head. From further back (B), smash the ball deep.

Let your right leg swing past left in scissor-like action when you hit ball

Meet ball above and in front of you at full racket-arm's reach

Jump off back leg to smash ball before it dips behind you

Once airborne, drop racket head into throwing position

After hitting up and over ball, land on left foot

84 FOOTWORK

To line up smashes quickly, you need to keep sideways-on to the ball as you position yourself behind and below the ball. Both the side-step and the cross-over will get you in the right position. Footwork for the side-step is simple, but the cross-over needs practice.

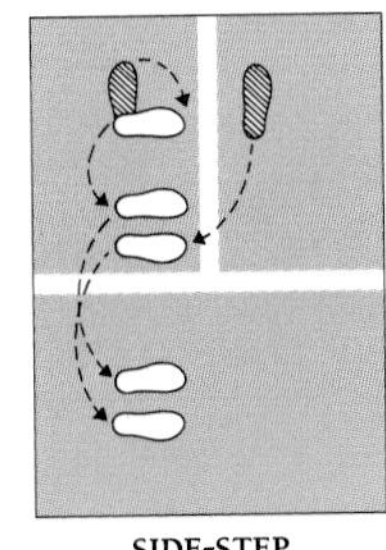

SIDE-STEP

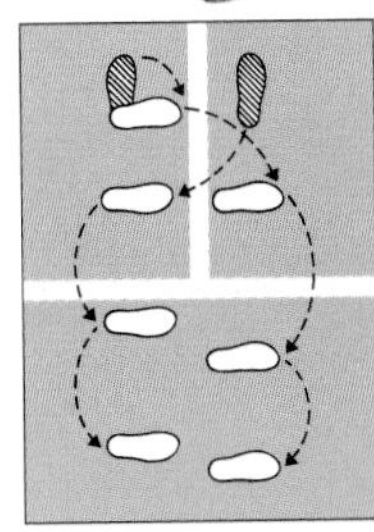

CROSS-OVER

85 The point-up

Pivot sideways-on, bending your elbow to lift the racket head as you extend your other arm to point up at your opponent's lob. Keep pointing up as you position yourself to smash the ball. By pointing up longer you will be able to time your smash perfectly.

- Your left arm plays a vital role, for not only does it help you to keep the ball in front of you as you track back, but it also measures half the distance your racket-wielding arm can reach.

Straighten left arm and point up at falling ball
Look up along arm at ball
Keep elbow high and racket poised to drop into throwing position
Place feet shoulder-width apart for stability

Overhead View
Point up at the ball as you turn, bringing the racket in across your shoulders before dropping it deep into the throwing position.

86 THE HIT

Fully extend your racket arm as you throw your racket head up to meet the ball, with the full face of the racket strings. Hit the ball out in front of you and finish the stroke like the service. Your back foot will stabilize you at impact. Start with the Modified Eastern grip and progress as you gain experience to the Continental grip.

Hit ball ahead of you at racket-arm's reach

Turn playing shoulder powerfully into the hit

Stretch and incline whole body

Balance your body with weight forwards and legs straight

Get up on tiptoes at impact

FULL STRETCH
In action at full stretch, the player meets the ball in front of him. As in serving, the left arm helps to direct force upwards.

87 SMASH TACTICS

The smash can only be used against lobs or high-bouncing balls, so develop an attacking game that forces your opponent to put up a defensive lob. Aim for his backhand corner. High lobs should be smashed after the bounce, but use a jump-smash for balls you would not otherwise reach. Inside the service line, angle smashes to the sidelines.

APPROACH PLAY

88 APPROACH SHOTS

In approaching the net, the placement of your shots is crucial to the success of any attack. Allow your position and the height at which you play the ball to dictate the stroke, but shorten the take-back for extra control. Once in the forecourt, use your volleying skills.

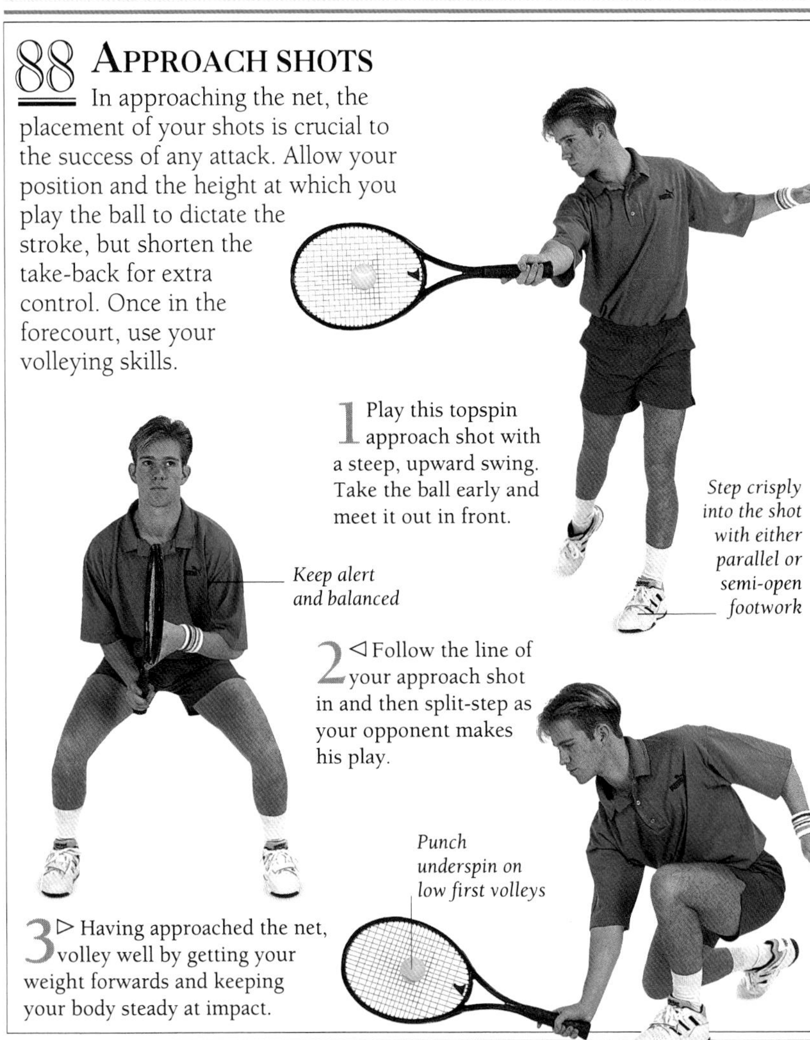

Keep alert and balanced
Step crisply into the shot with either parallel or semi-open footwork
Punch underspin on low first volleys

1 Play this topspin approach shot with a steep, upward swing. Take the ball early and meet it out in front.

2 ◁ Follow the line of your approach shot in and then split-step as your opponent makes his play.

3 ▷ Having approached the net, volley well by getting your weight forwards and keeping your body steady at impact.

89 APPROACH TACTICS

The basic rule of approach tactics is never to approach the net from a deep position. Aim to get where you want to be before your opponent strikes. If this is not possible, split-step early. The court *(right)* shows the areas of play. The dark blue area is advisable, the mid-blue possible, but it is too risky to make an approach shot from the pale blue area. It is better to move behind the baseline and wait for a real opportunity to present itself.

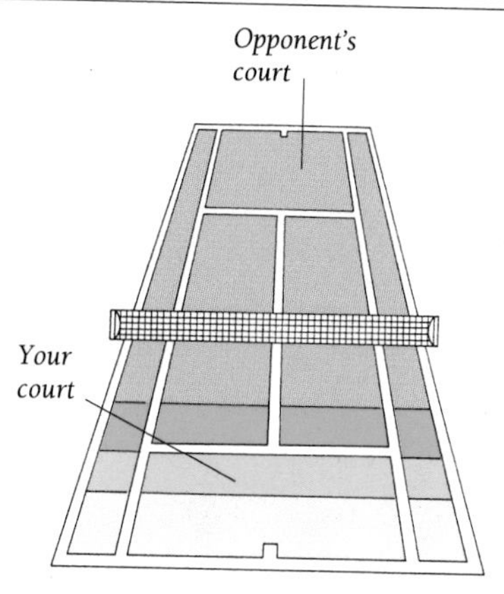
Opponent's court
Your court

90 SPLIT-STEPPING OPTIONS

Split-stepping is simply interrupting your forward run by planting your feet shoulder-width apart in order to gain a mobile ready position. Split-step early in order to be perfectly balanced for instant lateral movement to respond to your opponent's return shot. By split-stepping, you can read that shot and be better able to move quickly to your right to cut off your opponent's cross-court return, or to your left to backhand volley an attempted passing shot down-the-line.

Step to right and punch the ball
React and move in response to opponent's shot
Step to left to meet ball in front
FOREHAND RESPONSE
READY POSITION
BACKHAND RESPONSE

91 SERVING & VOLLEYING

The serve-and-volley is a decisive tactic that can give you control of the net area. As with approach shots, it is accuracy, pace, and depth of service that dictate subsequent volleying success. Give yourself time to reach a good volleying position by serving at three-quarters' speed to your opponent's weaker stroke, applying slice for extra control. Serve-and-volley success relies heavily on basic volleying techniques, so always focus on the ball, react early, and play forwards, getting your weight behind every shot.

Cut around right side of ball to apply slice to serve

1 Take up your service stance and select your service type and direction.

Keep wrist firm and racket at wrist level

3 △ After split-stepping, get well down, stepping across and sitting-in to those low first volleys.

Split-step early and be ready to move laterally

2 ◁ Try to cross the service line before split-stepping as your opponent makes his play.

THE GAME OF TENNIS

92 RULES OF THE GAME

Always play tennis by the rules. Toss a coin to decide who serves first. Serve from behind your baseline, starting in the right court for the first point, the left for the second. The service ball must be struck before it bounces, and must go over the net and land in the service court diagonally opposite. If you serve a fault you can serve again, but a double-fault gives your opponent the point. A receiver cannot volley the serve or let it bounce twice.

THE UMPIRE
The umpire sits in a high chair above the court to see that fair play and the rules of the game are observed.

93 PROGRESSIVE PLAYING

First and foremost, tennis is a game of control. It also requires consistency, depth, and power.

- Develop control by improving your tracking or receiving skills, so that you can move quickly and position yourself correctly in order to time the ball perfectly, be it a simple return or the best shot you will ever play in your life!
- As your timing improves, you must aim to be more consistent by not making unforced errors.
- After consistency, depth of shot must be added to your repertoire to keep your opponent away from the net and pinned in the backcourt.
- Finally, to dictate or counter your opponent's attack, bring power to your play by developing increased momentum through biomechanical principles (*see p.19*).

94 TACTICS ON COURT

Tactically, the area behind and up to your baseline is the backcourt, the area on the court between your service line and the net is the forecourt, and the area in between is no-man's-land. If you have to play a shot in no-man's-land, play it and get out fast or you may be caught with the ball at your feet and no time to play the next shot.

- Your main tactical aims are to keep the ball in play, to make your opponent run, to wrong-foot your opponent by disguising your intentions, and to play on his or her weaknesses by varying each shot.

CENTREPOINT TACTIC
Having reached a safe centrepoint in the forecourt, the attacking player moves out to cut off an attempted pass with a low volley.

95 CENTREPOINT AWARENESS

The centrepoint is midway between the two extremes of your opponent's return. It is a good tactic to ensure that your next centrepoint is close to you, but there is a danger of being caught out on your way there. This need not happen if you ease up when your opponent is playing the ball. In this example, the server plays a wide service to the receiver, who replies with a deep cross-court return (red) so that his next centrepoint is in between the server's possible shots (blue). If the receiver had chosen to play down-the-line, his next centrepoint would have been well beyond the centre mark.

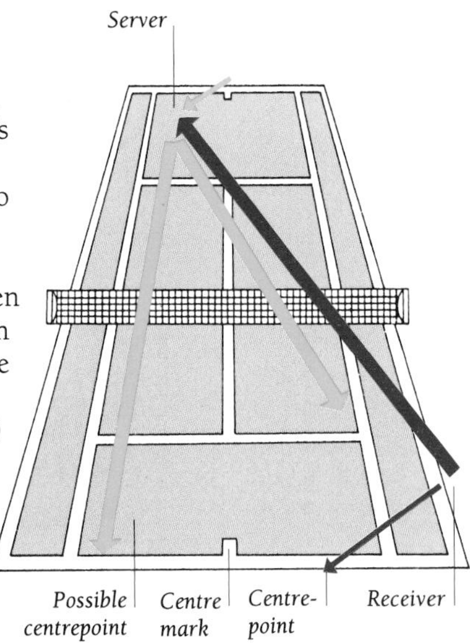

96 PERCENTAGE PLAY

Percentage play is about playing the safest shots that provide you with the greatest margin for error. As the court is longer diagonally and the net lower in the middle, it makes sense to hit most shots cross-court with height and depth. Tactically, choose the shot that is easiest for you to play, even if you've already played it five times in that rally. Your opponent may become impatient and attempt the more difficult down-the-line shot on the next ball.

97 PLAYING DOUBLES

In contrast to the singles game, doubles is about team work, and you must play together. Try to play level with your partner, aiming to get to the net quickly and remain there until you have won the point. If you are in doubt about placing a shot during a rally, aim between your opponents, thus possibly creating confusion about which one of them should play the ball. A successful doubles team places far more emphasis on team work and tactics than on the sheer physical strength associated with singles.

A QUICK INTERCEPT
A ball aimed diagonally between your opponents is always wise, but an alert net player may intercept it with a volley.

98 DOUBLES TACTICS

The court area per player in doubles is smaller than in singles. Because the aim of all four players is to get to the net, it is essential to get at least 75 per cent of your first serves into court. Sacrifice speed but maintain depth and accuracy.

- When receiving, keep your returns low over the net, unless you are lobbing, and aim 80 per cent of them cross-court, away from the server's partner at the net.
- If following in behind your service or return is too difficult, play a groundstroke before advancing.
- The server's partner should cover towards the middle to help the server's net approach.

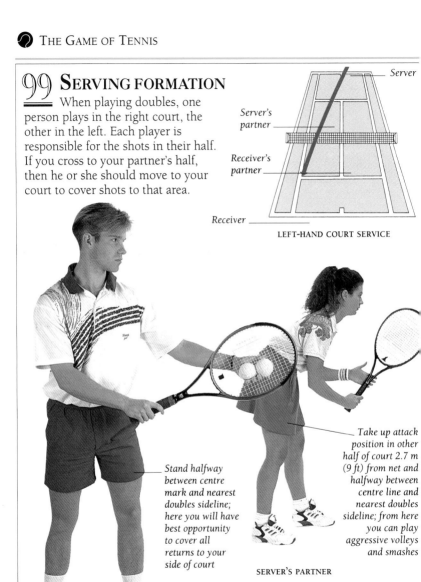

99 SERVING FORMATION

When playing doubles, one person plays in the right court, the other in the left. Each player is responsible for the shots in their half. If you cross to your partner's half, then he or she should move to your court to cover shots to that area.

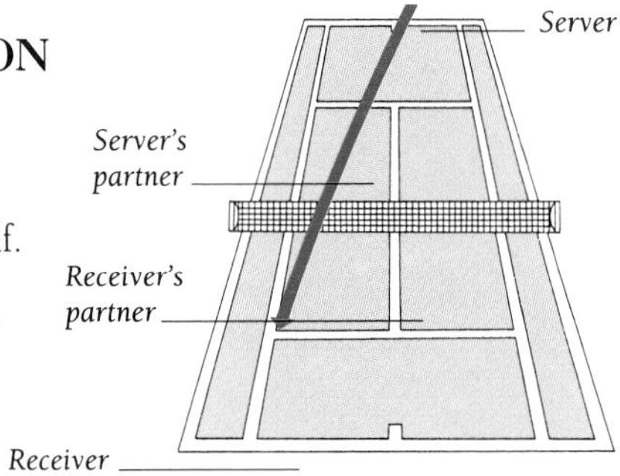

LEFT-HAND COURT SERVICE

Take up attack position in other half of court 2.7 m (9 ft) from net and halfway between centre line and nearest doubles sideline; from here you can play aggressive volleys and smashes

SERVER'S PARTNER

Stand halfway between centre mark and nearest doubles sideline; here you will have best opportunity to cover all returns to your side of court

SERVER

100 RECEIVING FORMATION

When receiving, start from the baseline area with your partner in mid-court. Having decided who receives in which court, keep these positions for the set. The receiver's partner should be able to advance to the net or retreat behind the baseline, as well as counter-volley if the server's partner intercepts your partner's return.

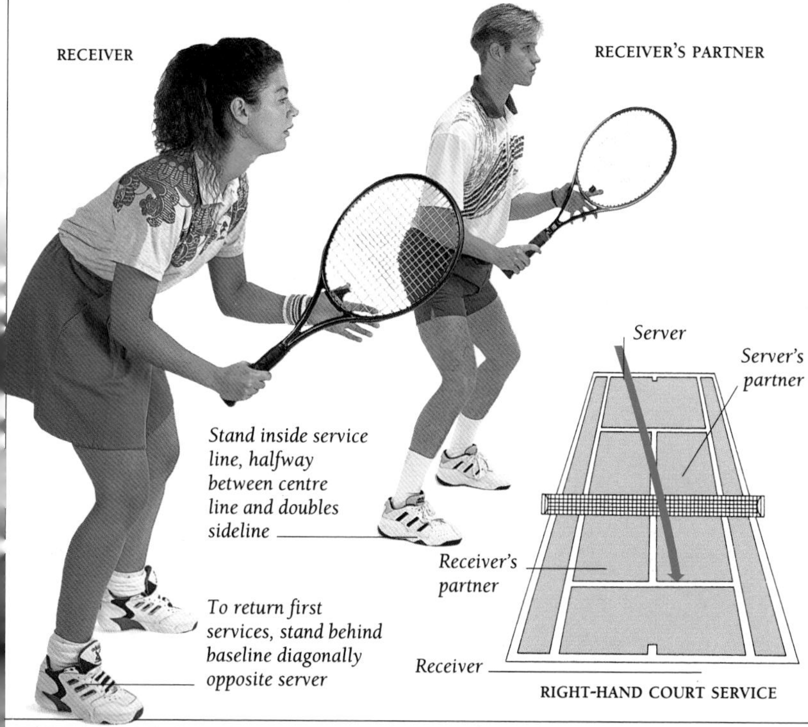

RECEIVER

RECEIVER'S PARTNER

Stand inside service line, halfway between centre line and doubles sideline

To return first services, stand behind baseline diagonally opposite server

Server

Server's partner

Receiver's partner

Receiver

RIGHT-HAND COURT SERVICE

101 CHOOSING A PARTNER

Try playing with different partners until you find a player whose game complements your own. Being friends off the court can help you establish on-court rapport.

- If you prefer playing in the right court, find a partner who likes playing in the left, and vice-versa.
- Make sure that you both share the same ideas about tactics.

INDEX

Acknowledgments

Paul Douglas & Dorling Kindersley would like to thank Hilary Bird for compiling the index; Ann Kay for proof-reading; Mark Bracey for computer assistance; Alan Douglas, Craig Douglas, Ross McCue, and Melissa Traub for modelling; Pro Kennex (UK) Ltd of Wooburn Green, Bucks., First Service of Cobham, Surrey, and Sport & Ski of Woking Surrey, for supplying equipment; and the Hampshire Tennis & Health Club, West End, Southampton, and the Chris Lane Tennis & Health Club, Surrey, for location photography.

Photography
All photography by Tim Ridley, Nick Goodall, and Matthew Ward, except for Colorsport, p.65, and Robert Harding Picture Library, p.67.

Illustration
Craig Austin, Paul Dewhurst, Janos Marrfy, Pete Sargent, and Rob Shone.